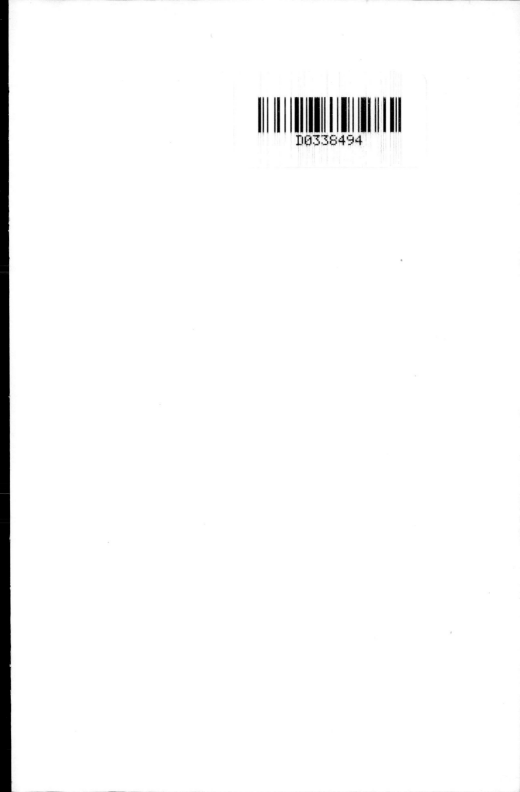
D0338494

THE THINGS THAT MATTER

By the same author

Whatever's Happening to Women?

THE THINGS THAT MATTER

An Anthology of Women's Spiritual Poetry

Edited and Introduced by
JULIA NEUBERGER

St. Martin's Press
New York

THE THINGS THAT MATTER. Collection, introduction, and notes copyright ©
1992 by Julia Neuberger. All rights reserved. Printed in the United States of
America. No part of this book may be used or reproduced in any manner
whatsoever without written permission except in the case of brief quotations
embodied in critical articles or reviews. For information, address St. Martin's
Press, 175 Fifth Avenue, New York, N.Y. 10010.

Library of Congress Cataloging-in-Publication Data

The things that matter : an anthology of women's spiritual poetry /
    Julia Neuberger, editor.
        p.   cm.
    "A Thomas Dunne book."
    ISBN 0-312-11899-6
    1. Women—Religious life—Poetry.   2. Religious poetry, English—
Women authors.   3. Religious poetry, American—Women authors.
I. Neuberger, Julia.
PR1191.T45   1995
821.008′0382′082—dc20   94-46616
                                                                CIP

First published in Great Britain by Kyle Cathie Limited

First U.S. Edition: April 1995
10 9 8 7 6 5 4 3 2 1

CONTENTS

ACKNOWLEDGEMENTS

Every effort has been made to trace copyright holders of material in this book. The Editors and Publishers apologize if any material has been included without permission and would be glad to be told of anyone who has not been consulted.

The Editor and Publisher wish to thank the following for permission to quote copyright material:

Elizabeth Barnett, literary executor for 'The Anguish', 'What's This of Death', 'I See So Clearly Now My Similar Years', 'Life, Were Thy Pains as are the Pains of Hell', 'God's World' and 'Siege' by Edna St. Vincent Millay. Copyright © 1917, 1923, 1928, 1945, 1951, 1955 by Edna St. Vincent Millay and Norma Millay Ellis.

A & C Black for 'Pallor' by A. Mary Robinson.

Carcanet Press Ltd for 'Christmas Carols' by Patricia Beer and 'Wine Bowl' by H.D. (Hilda Doolittle).

Centaur Press for 'The Other Journey' by Katharine Garrison Chapin.

Curtis Brown, London for 'The Dream' copyright Vita Sackville-West, on behalf of the author's estate.

Dodd Mead for 'Gandhi' by Angela Morgan.

Enitharmon Press for 'The Sparrow's Skull' and 'Lame Arm' by Ruth Pitter.

Faber and Faber Ltd for 'Choosing a Name' and 'At Richmond' by Anne Ridler and 'Mystic' by Sylvia Plath.

Farrar Strauss & Giroux, Inc. for 'Seascape' by Elizabeth Bishop. Copyright © 1979, 1983 by Alice Helen Methfessel and 'Last Hill in a Vista' by Louise Bogan. Copyright © 1968 by Louise Bogan.

Alfred A. Knopf Inc for 'Duet', 'Let Not My Death Be Long' and 'Protest' by Leonora Speyer.

Harcourt, Brace, Jovanovich for 'Height' by Anne Morrow Lindbergh.

David Higham Associates for 'Still Falls the Rain' by Edith Sitwell.

Houghton Mifflin Company for 'Patterns' by Amy Lowell. Copyright © 1955 by Houghton Mifflin Company. Copyright renewed 1983 by Houghton Mifflin Company, Brinton P. Roberts, and G. D'andelot Belin, Esquire. All rights reserved.

Indiana University Press for 'Ain't I A Woman?', adapted by Erlene Stetson from the speech by Sojourner Truth.

Mrs Leonie Troy for 'Early Waking' and 'Those Not Elect' by Leonie Adams.

H. Vinal for 'The Day You Went' by Beatrice Ravenel.

Virago Press for 'I Do Not Speak'; 'Come Death (1)' and 'Come Death (2)' by Stevie Smith.

The Trustees of her Will Trust for 'The Buried Child' by Dorothy Wellesley.

INTRODUCTION

The reader may find the list of poets whose works are included in this volume strange, for some of their names are well known, even fashionable, and their poems are in print elsewhere. But the whole area of women's spiritual poetry has been badly neglected. All the great anthologies of spiritual and religious poetry are dominated by men. The works of Donne, Herbert and Traherne, of Keats and Wordsworth, of Tennyson and Robert Southey, are well represented. Much of the writing of nineteenth-century women poets has been dismissed throughout this century as sentimental, unprepossessing, dull and poorly formed. Such of those women's works as are still read are not usually those which are spiritual in tone, although that genre may well have formed the bulk of their writing. Indeed, it would not be unfair to say that there is a whole raft of literature out there which has been largely disregarded, especially in Britain.

Thus most of the poets in this volume are barely known, and the main reason for that is their gender. Most anthologies of poetry, unless compiled within the last ten to twenty years, have relatively few females within them. They will have plenty of second-rate men, and even second-rate poems by first-rate male poets, but the number of women writers represented will be tiny and what appears will usually be a tiny selection of their work. The Penguin *Poetry of the Thirties*, edited by Robin Skelton and published in 1964, is a typical example. It has only Anne Ridler amongst its otherwise entirely male authors, when it could have had Edith Sitwell, Kathleen Raine and Vita Sackville-West, to name but a few distinguished females who were writing good poetry in that decade. Such omissions tell us a great deal about the male anthologisers and critics who simply did not bother, at some stages of history, to listen for a different note in the music, a different voice.

American anthologies are a little better. The Victorian anthologies are full of female writers, though some of those produced in the Thirties, Forties and Fifties have a remarkable dearth of them.

Honourable exceptions can be made for Nicholson and Lee's *Oxford Book of English Mystical Verse* (1927) and Markham's *The Book of American Poetry* (1926), but they are unusual. The pity of it is that all these overlooked women writers have important messages for the reader interested in the inner life, and particularly the contemplation of death and immortality. Early this century, Victorian women's poetry was disregarded by male critics because they felt it was uninteresting or just not very good. More recently, the spiritual poetry has had a cool reception from feminist critics because of its private, unassertive nature and also because they find some of the Victorian sentimentality hard to take. Yet even if we acknowledge the difficulties of the sentimentality and admit that some women poets have produced work that is less than first rate, there are in amongst it all some gems of fine writing and some penetrating insights.

The finest works of the less well-known writers here – most of which have hitherto been neglected, ignored or despised – are worthy to appear alongside the writings of the few famous poets included in this volume. One of the best known is Emily Dickinson, whose works, with their mystical quality and haunting air of secretiveness, still capture our imaginations a century after her death. Emily Brontë's poetry has always been nearly as popular as her best known work, *Wuthering Heights*. On the other hand, although the novels of her sisters, Charlotte and Anne, are familiar classics, their poetry is only lately being rediscovered. Elizabeth Barrett Browning is probably more famous for her real-life love story than for her verse. Similarly, Christina Rossetti is remembered for her refusal to marry for religious reasons, but her poetry is barely read nowadays, having been regarded as sentimental, and, in many cases – most unfairly – as second rate.

The Victorian women poets shared an obsession with death that sat uncomfortably with mid-twentieth-century perceptions and inhibitions. As this century draws to a close, however, and the discussion of death becomes more acceptable, it is legitimate to show an interest in poetry and prose that view the prospect of one's own passing with romantic hope, or with morbid curiosity. Intermingled with this we find maudlin certainty and a fair dollop of sentimentality. But the sentiment, of which there is much in both Elizabeth Barrett Browning and Christina Rossetti, should not mask the true faith these women held, nor make us insensitive to the doubts they had, and the fears. Their voices are not as naked or as compelling as Emily Brontë's at her best, nor as haunting as Emily Dickinson's. But they repay study, and in Christina Rossetti particularly there are clear tensions between her theological certainties and her personal faith.

The obsession with death is worth exploring a little further. The imagination runs riot over the details of the death. Emily Dickinson describes 'Death' as being

> like the insect
> Menacing the tree

while Charlotte Mew, in her powerful poem 'In Nunhead Cemetery', writes of 'This morning, after *that* was carried out.' Adelaide Crapsey, largely unknown to English readers, is almost reminiscent of Emily Dickinson when she writes:

> These be
> Three silent things:
> The falling snow ... the hour
> Before the dawn ... the mouth of one
> Just dead.

And she anticipates her own, lonely death – cold, dark, lain out on the bed, with the sheet drawn under her chin.

It is no surprise that death preoccupies these women so. Many of them would have seen friends, family members, children, die, and there would have been no detached, medical attitude to death. It was a family affair. To die alone was more unusual, more disgraceful, perhaps. 'The good death', that essentially eighteenth-century concept, would have been a familiar idea to the nineteenth-century poets, and they would have seen endless pictures of the death of children, bathed in a golden light, or of adults, surrounded by family and friends, shriven, confessed, at peace, still, pain-free or with pain overcome by faith.

For the Brontës, death was a regular visitor, as one sister after another succumbed to consumption. Elizabeth Barrett Browning was an invalid when Robert Browning met her, and used to the delicacy expected of a young woman not expected to live long. (In fact, she lived to be fifty-five, considerably older than any of the Brontës.) Consumption was a familiar killer, particularly of women, and death in and around childbirth was commonplace. So these women saw a lot of death, and wrote about it, and anticipated it, in a way that is hard for us to grasp. We who are twentieth-century people do not have the vocabulary to deal with death, as they did, and we find the sentiments so freely expressed in this volume hard to share.

Yet in Western society our views of death are changing. The hospice movement, the Macmillan nurses, the whole question of pain relief, have all made it a legitimate subject of conversation again. Much of the discussion is about the physical aspects of death, about weakness, pain and the impoverishment of life. But increasingly the spiritual aspects are being touched on as well, as the hospice movement makes it clear that its approach is holistic – that the whole person, spiritual and physical, is taken care of. So with renewed late-twentieth-century eyes we can go into the poetry of the nineteenth century, written by women of faith and passion, facing their own and their loved ones' mortality, with more understanding than we would have given it in previous years.

To add to that, we have a new appreciation of mystical poetry. There is a fervour in the imagination of Emily Dickinson or Adelaide Crapsey, and a fear, and a ghostliness, that appeals to the still sensitised minds of the late twentieth century, where belief in ghosts is on the increase, and religious faith, despite many strongly held opinions to the contrary, remains an important part of the world view for just over half the population.

That sense of the existence of the 'other' – be it ghosts, spirits or the divine – is ever present in the poems assembled here. Leonie Adams, for instance, who is still writing, talks in 'Early Waking' of 'No time to raise that lively ghost'. Emily Brontë's vivid sense of the other brings the lines:

> And slumber mould my misery
> Into some strange and spectral dream,

Whose phantom horrors made me know
The worst extent of human woe.

In 'Human Life's Mystery', Elizabeth Barrett Browning has 'Things nameless!' which, she continues,

In passing so,
Do stroke us with a subtle grace;
We say, 'Who passes?' – They are dumb;
We cannot see them go or come,
Their touches fall soft, cold, as snow
Upon a blind man's face.

Mary Coleridge has her picture of 'some accursed thing', and Theodosia Garrison writes of 'the three ghosts on the lonesome road'. This is no coincidence. It is not by chance that all these writers have spirits and ghosts in their vocabulary and imagination. The supernatural forms part of their truly held belief, and though few have in mind nasty, ghost-like creatures popping out of the dark, there is a sense of 'other' in the loneliness of these women, in their preparedness for death, in the idea that there is some being, some person, some spirit present when they lie in bed at night or walk in the loneliest of places. One could argue that this is merely part of human sensibility, but in these poets I believe it to be more than that. It is, whether or not we the readers believe in ghosts or spirits ourselves, a *heightened* sensibility, perhaps a feeling of closeness to nature, or a sense that the writers are not alone, but not sure who or what is with them, that leads to figures best described as spirits or ghosts appearing in their poetry.

There is, too, an orthodox religiosity, almost entirely Christian, that speaks of spirits, and a great proportion of the poetry gathered here is profoundly Christian. Leading figures in this respect are Anne Brontë, whose poetry is almost theological in many cases, battling as it does with Calvinist doctrine; Eva Gore-Booth, Harriet Eleanor Hamilton-King and Alice Meynell. Alice Meynell converted to Catholicism around 1870, when she was in her twenties, and her poetry reflects this in great detail. Poems such as 'To the Mother of Christ the Son of Man', and 'Via, et Veritas, et Vita' display that all too clearly, but there is also her 'Saint Catherine of Siena', which she heads with 'Written for Strephon, who said that a woman must lean, or she should not have his chivalry.' As she gently satirises that masculine attitude, Meynell's Catholicism and her feminism are mixed in equal measure.

That feminist element is another unifying feature of much of this poetry: specifically, there is a recognition of women's role in religion, publicly denied. It ranges from the explicit in Frances E. W. Harper's 'Vashti', the story of the wife of the King of Persia, Ahasuerus, who refused to unveil her face in front of her husband's friends, and walked out on him, to Alice Meynell's gentler correction of male perceptions. It includes Kathleen Millay's magnificent 'The Masterpiece', about the creation of woman; Emily Pfeiffer's appeal, 'A Protest', to women to combat new taxes and oppression of the poor; and most magnificent of them all, Sojourner Truth's 'Ain't I a Woman?'. Sojourner Truth was a freed slave, and her language of liberty, of being both black and female, is powerful and moving.

Set against that is Christina Rossetti's surprising acceptance of the place accorded to women by the Christian church, derived from St Paul's dictum of keeping the women silent, learning with all subjection. Instead of the protest, explicit or even implicit in the didactic style of her verse, she writes:

> Let woman fear to teach and bear to learn,
> Remembering the first woman's first mistake.
> Eve had for pupil the inquiring snake,
> Whose doubts she answered on a great concern,
> But the tables so contrived to turn,
> It next was his to give and hers to take;
> Till man deemed poison sweet for her sweet sake,
> And fired a train by which the world must burn.

There is little more orthodox in thought than that to be found in Christian writings. Eve is seen here as the cause of the Fall from Grace, and there is no questioning of the theology, or consideration of man's blameworthiness, or of whether it was not man's weakness, rather than woman's temptation, which caused Adam to sin.

The American poets show a greater social conscience altogether, and are more clearly feminist and politicised. This is at least partly because of the movement for the emancipation of slaves, and a part of that was caught up with early campaigns for women's rights. But it is also a different style of writing, be it Katharine Lee Bates' fury at the execution of Sarah Threeneedles in Boston in 1698, and at the intolerance of the religious leaders of the community, or Charlotte Perkins Gilman on 'Child Labor'. Add to that Angela Morgan's 'Gandhi', with its reverence for the man as a bringer of peace, and Lola Ridge's 'Sons of Belial', with its condemnation of the death of Rosa Luxemburg and of the lynching of blacks in Missouri, and there is a note in the music very different from that to be found in the English poets. At the same time, the consciousness of slavery and its wrongs is found in Elizabeth Barrett Browning's moving 'The Runaway Slave at Pilgrim's Point', although here the case is made to appeal to our sympathies, rather than to evoke our anger.

But of all the motifs running throughout these poems, the puzzle of human suffering, the nearness of death and the love and fear of the divine predominate. Harriet Eleanor Hamilton-King states in 'The Disciples' that

> We suffer. Why we suffer – that is hid
> With God's foreknowledge in the clouds of Heaven.

In 'Patterns', Amy Lowell records the suffering of a woman discovering just before her marriage that her lover has been killed in battle:

> For the man who should loose me is dead,
> Fighting with the Duke of Flanders,
> In a pattern called war.

And then she cries out in agony:

> Christ! What are patterns for?

Charlotte Mew records suffering in her 'Song': 'Sorrow, sorrow, is my bed.' And one of the most moving accounts of human suffering is that of Edith Nesbit in her poem 'After Death', in which, having run

through the horrors of a loved one's death, she ends with the line:
'Thank God, thank God, that it was you who died.'

Death is never far away, with Edna St Vincent Millay's 'What's this
of death, from you who will never die?' and Emily Pfeiffer's 'The "Sting
of Death"', with its assertion of death's pain, but love's triumph. There
is A. Mary F. Robinson's 'Pallor', with its description of the angels as

> pale –
> For all have died, when all is said,
> Nor shall the lutes of Eden avail
> To let them dream they are not dead.

There is hope of immortality in Christina Rossetti's 'Remember' and
'The End of Time', but a very different welcome to death and
disaffection from life in Stevie Smith's two poems entitled 'Come,
Death'. For her, life was not a great bonus. 'Foolish illusion, what has
Life to give?', and her cry is to 'Sweet Death':

> You are the only god
> Who comes as a servant when he is called, you know . . .
> Come death, do not be slow.

But of all the poems in this volume about death, the anger and
assertions of cruelty in Emily Brontë's 'Death' and the apparent
certainty of eternity in that poem and in 'Faith and Despondency' most
move the modern reader. Here is a young woman, facing death in her
family and in herself, with a strong Christian conviction, probably with
the knowledge that if she moved from her beloved home death could
be averted or at least delayed, writing of inevitability and of passion, of
faith and despair, and making death no stranger, but a fact of her life
and sometimes almost a friend. That attitude, in that fine verse, is
foreign to us and yet appealing, and it is the key to a mood different
from that most commonly expressed in our era, but one for which we
can have great sympathy and admiration.

Reading these poems was, for me, a glimpse into what has become
almost a secret life. Here is deep spirituality, sometimes intense
religiosity or a passionate anger about social injustice. Here, too, is a

lyrical delight in the English language as it deals with some of the most inexpressible of ideas. These are women's voices, different from men's in their quest. Some of these poets had what we might describe as a conventional religious approach. Some had undergone conversion experiences, while others were not formally religious at all. But in each case there is an individuality about their grappling, and an intensity of experience, often in the privacy of their own homes, that is moving and joyful. Though we can rail at the wasted talents of so many of them, dying before their time, accepting their fate, nevertheless the anticipation of that experience evokes some of the finest poetry of this collection.

CAROLINE SOUTHEY
1786–1854

Caroline Southey was the second wife of the poet Robert Southey, and is also known by her maiden name of Caroline Bowles. She was never a particularly distinguished poet, though Robert Southey, long before he became her husband, had treated her kindly and tried to help her publish her works, when she was left alone in the world and tried to make a living by her pen. Her father's adopted son, Colonel Bruce, gave her an allowance of £150 a year, but this was not enough to enable her to live in the cottage she inherited from her father, Buckland Cottage in the New Forest. It was there she lived for most of her life, apart from the four years she spent as the wife of Robert Southey, whose interest in her eventually led to a proposal of marriage when he was in fast-failing health. Whether she realised how ill he was is never clear. Suffice it to say that within three months of their marriage he was losing his faculties, and she had to live with his children, who loathed her and made her life hell. When Southey died, he left her £2000, but this did not make up for the loss of Captain Bruce's annuity, which she had forfeited on her marriage. Indeed, it was only a small crown pension conferred upon her in 1852 that saved her from financial ruin.

Caroline Southey ended her days in the New Forest as she had begun, and is buried in Lymington churchyard. Because she remained on friendly terms with Robert Southey's daughter, Edith Warter, who did not live with him, and her husband, she left the Warters much of her correspondence with Southey, which they published. That reveals her as a witty and satirical woman, qualities which do not appear in her poetry. Nevertheless, her poems were popular in her day, and some of them, such as her 'Chapters on Churchyards', or 'Tales of the Factories' make fine reading still. Her talents lie in her story-telling and her passionate campaigning, as well as her felicitous near-prose style when at her best.

To Death

Come not in terrors clad, to claim
  An unresisting prey:
Come like an evening shadow, Death!
  So stealthily, so silently!
And shut mine eyes, and steal my breath
  Then willingly, O willingly,
    With thee I'll go away!

What need to clutch with iron grasp
  What gentlest touch may take?
What need with aspect dark to scare,
  So awfully, so terribly,
The weary soul would hardly care,
  Call'd quietly, call'd tenderly,
    From thy dread power to break?

'Tis not as when thou markest out
  The young, the blest, the gay,
The loved, the loving – they who dream
  So happily, so hopefully;
Then harsh thy kindest call may seem,
  And shrinkingly, reluctantly,
    The summon'd may obey.

But I have drunk enough of life –
  The cup assign'd to me
Dash'd with a little sweet at best,
  So scantily, so scantily –
To know full well that all the rest
  More bitterly, more bitterly,
    Drugg'd to the last will be.

And I may live to pain some heart
　　That kindly cares for me:
To pain, but not to bless. O Death!
　　Come quietly, come lovingly –
And shut mine eyes, and steal my breath;
　　Then willingly, O willingly,
　　　I'll go away with thee!

'I never cast a flower away'

I never cast a flower away,
　　The gift of one who cared for me –
A little flower – a faded flower –
　　But it was done reluctantly.

I never looked a last adieu
　　To things familiar, but my heart
Shrank with a feeling almost pain,
　　Even from their lifelessness to part.

I never spoke the word 'Farewell,'
　　But with an utterance faint and broken;
An earth-sick longing for the time
　　When it shall never more be spoken.

FELICIA HEMANS
1793–1835

Felicia Hemans was born in Liverpool in 1793, the daughter of an Irish
merchant, who was also Imperial and Tuscan Consul there at one time.
She had three brothers, all of whom had distinguished careers, largely

in the Peninsula Wars. After financial losses, the family left Liverpool for North Wales, where Felicia was educated by her mother. She started writing poetry at an early age and her parents published her *Poems* when she was fourteen. The volume met with criticism, but she recovered and wrote *England and Spain, or, Valour and Patriotism* soon afterwards. The poet Shelley read some of her work and longed to correspond with her. She refused, he persisted, and finally her mother had to intercede with some of his friends to make him stop writing!

In 1812 Felicia married Captain Hemans, an Irish gentleman, after a relationship that had already lasted three years, having started when she was fifteen. They had five sons, but afterwards parted. The rest of her life was taken up with the bringing up of her children, with writing, as her work became more and more popular, and a decline in her health. She received the Royal Society of Literature's prize in 1821, and gradually wrote more and more in defence of religion. Her poems were published in all the major magazines in Britain, and her reputation gradually extended to America, where she had at least one volume of verse published.

In 1831 she moved to Dublin where her second brother was Chief Commissioner of Police. There she succumbed to the ill-health which had troubled her for years, and she died in 1835. She is buried in St Anne's Church, Dublin.

Her poetry has often been criticised for its lack of depth. But although its excessive sentimentality may not be to modern taste, there are signs of a deep religiosity and sense of spiritual life.

A Father Reading the Bible

'Twas early day and sunlight stream'd
    Soft through a quiet room,
That hush'd, but not forsaken, seem'd,
    Still, but with nought of gloom.
For there, serene in happy age,
    Whose hope is from above,
A Father communed with the page
    Of Heaven's recorded love.

Pure fell the beam, and meekly bright,
On his gray holy hair,
And touched the page with tenderest light,
As if its shrine were there!
But oh! that patriarch's aspect shone
With something lovelier far –
A radiance all the spirit's own,
Caught not from sun or star.

Some word of life e'en then had met
His calm benignant eye;
Some ancient promise, breathing yet
Of immortality!
Some martyr's prayer, wherein the glow
Of quenchless faith survives:
While every feature said – 'I know
That my Redeemer lives!'

And silent stood his children by,
Hushing their very breath,
Before the solemn sanctity
Of thoughts o'ersweeping death.
Silent – yet did not each young breast
With love and reverence melt?
Oh! blest be those fair girls, and blest
That home where God is felt!

The Child's First Grief

'Oh! call my Brother back to me!
I cannot play alone;
The summer comes with flower and bee –
Where is my Brother gone?

'The butterfly is glancing bright
    Across the sunbeam's track;
I care not now to chase its flight –
    Oh! call my Brother back!

'The flowers run wild – the flowers we sow'd
    Around our garden tree;
Our vine is drooping with its load –
    Oh! call him back to me!'

'He could not hear thy voice, fair child,
    He may not come to thee;
The face that once like spring-time smiled
    On earth no more thou'lt see.

'A rose's brief bright life of joy,
    Such unto him was given;
Go – thou must play alone, my boy!
    Thy Brother is in heaven!'

'And has he left his birds and flowers,
    And must I call in vain?
And, through the long, long summer hours,
    Will he not come again?

'And by the brook, and in the glade,
    Are all our wanderings o'er?
Oh, while my Brother with me play'd,
    Would I had loved him more!'

To a Family Bible

What household thoughts around thee, as their shrine,
Cling reverently? – of anxious looks beguiled,
My mother's eyes, upon thy page divine,
Each day were bent – her accents gravely mild,

Breathed out thy love: whilst I, a dreamy child,
Wandered on breeze-like fancies oft away,
To some lone tuft of gleaming spring-flowers wild,
Some fresh-discover'd nook for woodland play,
Some secret nest: yet would the solemn Word
At times, with kindlings of young wonder heard,
    Fall on my wakened spirit, there to be
A seed not lost; – for which, in darker years,
O Book of Heaven! I pour, with grateful tears,
Heart blessings on the holy dead and thee!

SOJOURNER TRUTH
1797–1883

Sojourner Truth was born into slavery and known as Isabella. Freed by
the New York Emancipation Act of 1827, she left New York in 1843
with a bag of clothes and twenty-five cents and adopted the name by
which she is remembered. She travelled down the length of the east
coast giving performances for white audiences, who were fascinated by
her unusual stature, her wit and her singing voice. In 1850, she
launched an attack on the white population's apathy about slavery and
at the end of the Civil War she was appointed head councillor of
Freedman's village in Virginia. She devoted the rest of her life to
lecturing and campaigning for a decent lifestyle and land ownership
rights for former slaves and spent years collecting signatures for a
presentation to Congress. She died disillusioned by America and its
disregard for human rights and truth. Her petition had been shelved
and ignored.

Sojourner Truth herself is remembered as a very courageous and far-
sighted woman. The poem which follows was originally a speech made
at the Women's Rights Convention in Akron, Ohio, in 1852. No exact
copy exists, but this has been adapted to a poetic format by Erlene

Stetson from the copy in *Sojourner, God's Faithful Pilgrim* by Arthur Huff Fauset (Chapel Hill, University of North Carolina Press, 1938).

Ain't I a Woman?

That man over there say
    a woman needs to be helped into carriages
and lifted over ditches
    and to have the best place everywhere.
Nobody ever helped me into carriages
    or over mud puddles
        or gives me a best place . . .

And ain't I a woman?
    Look at me
Look at my arm!
    I have plowed and planted
and gathered into barns
    and no man could head me . . .
And ain't I a woman?
    I could work as much
and eat as much as a man –
    when I could get to it –
and bear the lash as well
    and ain't I a woman?
I have born thirteen children
    and seen most all sold into slavery
and when I cried out a mother's grief
    none but Jesus heard me . . .
And ain't I a woman?
    that little man in black there say
a woman can't have as much rights as a man
    cause Christ wasn't a woman
Where did your Christ come from?
    From God and a woman!
Man had nothing to do with him!

If the first woman God ever made
was strong enough to turn the world
upside down, all alone
together women ought to be able to turn it
rightside up again.

HARRIET MARTINEAU
1802–1876

Harriet Martineau was born in Norwich of an educated family whose finances were in disarray. The Martineaus scrimped and saved to educate their children, but their well-meaning discipline and the elder children's general roughness meant that Harriet's childhood was wearing and unenjoyable. However, she began to write and think early in life. She learned 'Paradise Lost' by heart at seven, and studied French and Latin at home and at school. It was at school that her deafness manifested itself; it grew worse in her teens, and by twenty she was distressed and withdrawn, so that her parents sent her to Bristol, where her aunt by marriage had a school.

She became a disciple of the unitarian minister of Bristol, Lant Carpenter, and read the Bible systematically, as well as other tracts. In 1821 she sent an article, 'Female Writers on Practical Divinity', to the *Monthly Repository*, the Unitarian magazine. It was accepted and much praised, even by her brother Thomas who advised her to give up darning stockings and take to literature.

Thomas died in 1824; Harriet's father suffered financial ruin in 1825–6 and died in 1826 leaving his family in poor circumstances. As finances grew worse, she decided to write more actively and competed for prizes for essays on the conversion of Catholics, Jews and Muslims, all of which she won. She then formed a partnership with a publisher, Charles Fox, to bring out her stories, which were becoming very popular. She reached the acme of her popularity in the early 1830s and began to make money and to meet literary London. She was friendly with the Wordsworths in the Lake District, and was invited to all the great houses.

At the same time, she wrote on poor law reform and on other social issues, and her trip to the United States in 1834 brought her back a confirmed abolitionist.

Her illness became worse, and she was prescribed mesmerism as a possible relief. So she went to be mesmerised, grew rapidly healthy again, and was thereafter committed to mesmerism as a treatment, even practising it occasionally herself. She wrote more and more on social reform, popularising the work of Bright, Mill and Atkinson, and continuing to write stories with a wide audience. But it is her relatively limited output of poetry that is of interest here. It is not as attractive as her stories or her campaigning essays, but it shows a deep religiosity and begins to reveal her own fears about the anti-Catholic cause, something which ultimately made her stop writing for *Household Words*, which had been a loyal employer, on the grounds it was unfair to Catholics.

After an unhealthy start, she lived to the then ripe age of seventy-four, and pursued a career that was far more successful than she would have believed possible in her early years. She is nonetheless remembered more for her social reforming zeal than for her writing.

'Arise, my soul! and urge thy flight'

I

Arise, my soul! and urge thy flight,
And fix thy view on God alone,
As eagles spring to meet the light,
And gaze upon the radiant sun.

As planets on and onward roll,
As streams pour forth their swelling tide,
Press on thy steady course, my soul,
Nor pause, nor stop, nor turn aside.

Planets and suns shall dim their fire;
  Earth, air, and sea, shall melt away;
But though each star of heaven expire,
  Thou may'st survive that awful day.

In life, in death, thy course hold on:
  Though nature's self in ruins lie,
Pause not till heaven-gate be won;
  Then rest; for there thou canst not die.

II
Beneath this starry arch
  Nought resteth or is still;
But all things hold their march,
  As if by one great will:
    Moves one, move all;
    Hark to the footfall!
    On, on, for ever!

Yon sheaves were once but seed:
Will ripens into deed.
As cave-drops swell the streams,
Day-thoughts feed nightly dreams;
And sorrow tracketh wrong,
As echo follows song.
    On, on, for ever!

By night, like stars on high,
  The hours reveal their train;
They whisper, and go by;
  I never watch in vain:
    Moves one, move all:
    Hark to the footfall!
    On, on, for ever!

They pass the cradle-head,
And there a promise shed;
They pass the moist new grave,
And bid rank verdure wave;
They bear through every clime
The harvests of all time,
    On, on, for ever!

III

All men are equal in their birth,
    Heirs of the earth and skies;
All men are equal when that earth
    Fades from their dying eyes.

All wait alike on Him whose power
    Upholds the life He gave;
The sage within his star-lit tower,
    The savage in his cave.

God meets the throngs that pay their vows
    In courts their hands have made;
And hears the worshipper who bows
    Beneath the plantain shade.

'Tis man alone who difference sees,
    And speaks of high and low,
And worships those and tramples these,
    While the same path they go.

Oh, let man hasten to restore
    To all their rights of love;
In power and wealth exult no more;
    In wisdom lowly move.

Ye great! renounce your earth-born pride;
    Ye low, your shame and fear:
Live as ye worship side by side;
    Your brotherhood revere.

ELIZABETH BARRETT BROWNING
1806–1861

From childhood, Elizabeth Barrett Browning was devoted to literature. Her earliest passions were Homer and Pope, and she became a considerable literary and linguistic scholar, knowing Latin, Greek, Hebrew, French, German and Italian from a relatively young age. Yet this was a girl who received no formal education at all, but picked up what she could along the way from her brother's tutor. She wrote a premature epic of the Battle of Marathon in 1819, which her father had privately printed, but it was her later poems, published in 1844, which caught the eye of Robert Browning, the rising star of British letters. He wrote to her, met her, and eventually proposed.

By this time Elizabeth was an invalid. She had fallen from her horse in 1821, and spent long years lying in a darkened room, writing her poetry for amusement. Her correspondence with Browning gave her new life, and her health improved by leaps and bounds, making marriage a serious possibility. But her father, who ruled as a despot in the family, refused to permit it. Elizabeth and Robert eventually married in secret and travelled to France and Italy where their son was born in 1849, at the Casa Guidi in Florence.

They ran a hospitable house where authors and poets of all kinds found a welcome. Nathaniel Hawthorne wrote of Mrs Browning's pale, eager face and slender hands. She had charm and wit, and a profound religious faith, but, despite the near-miraculous recovery that had enabled her to marry, her health was never robust, and it failed her entirely in 1861, when she died. By that time she was world-renowned as a poet, with a passionate commitment to Italy's independence from Austria and to the emancipation of slaves. Although her first loves were husband, son and home, that domesticity barely appears in her poetry, now singularly unfashionable, with its religious orthodoxy and lack of humour. Nevertheless, it repays reading, for her crafting is skilled and her message of faith and hope, from an invalid with new life, a remarkable one.

The Weeping Saviour

HYMN III

'– tell
Whether His countenance can thee affright,
Tears in His eyes quench the amazing light.'
Donne

When Jesus' friend had ceased to be,
  Still Jesus' heart its friendship kept –
'Where have ye laid him?' – 'Come and see!'
  But ere His eyes could see, they wept.

Lord! not in sepulchres alone,
  Corruption's worm is rank and free;
The shroud of death our bosoms own –
  The shades of sorrow! Come and see!

Come, Lord! God's image cannot shine
  Where sin's funereal darkness lowers –
Come! turn those weeping eyes of Thine
  Upon these sinning souls of ours!

And let those eyes, with shepherd care,
  Their moving watch above us keep;
Till love the strength of sorrow wear,
  And as Thou weepedst, *we* may weep!

For surely we may weep to know,
  So dark and deep our spirit's stain;
That had Thy blood refused to flow,
  Thy very tears had flowed in vain.

The Runaway Slave at Pilgrim's Point

I stand on the mark beside the shore
  Of the first white pilgrim's bended knee,
Where exile turned to ancestor,
  And God was thanked for liberty.
I have run through the night, my skin is as dark,
I bend my knee down on this mark:
  I look on the sky and the sea.

O pilgrim-souls, I speak to you!
  I see you come proud and slow
From the land of the spirits pale as dew
  And round me and round me ye go.
O pilgrims, I have gasped and run
All night long from the whips of one
  Who in your names works sin and woe!

And thus I thought that I would come
  And kneel here where ye knelt before,
And feel your souls around me hum
  In undertone to the ocean's roar;
And lift my black face, my black hand,
Here, in your names, to curse this land
  Ye blessed in freedom's, evermore.

I am black, I am black,
  And yet God made me, they say:
But if He did so, smiling back
  He must have cast His work away
Under the feet of His white creatures,
With a look of scorn, that the dusky features
  Might be trodden again to clay.

And yet He has made dark things
    To be glad and merry as light:
There's a little dark bird sits and sings,
    There's a dark stream ripples out of sight,
And the dark frogs chant in the safe morass,
And the sweetest stars are made to pass
    O'er the face of the darkest night.

But *we* who are dark, we are dark!
    Ah God, we have no stars!
About our souls in care and cark
    Our blackness shuts like prison-bars:
The poor souls crouch so far behind
That never a comfort can they find
    By reaching through the prison-bars.

Indeed we live beneath the sky,
    That great smooth Hand of God stretched out
On all His children fatherly,
    To save them from the dread and doubt
Which would be if, from this low place,
All opened straight up to His face
    Into the grand eternity.

And still God's sunshine and His frost,
    They make us hot, they make us cold,
As if we were not black and lost;
    And the beasts and birds, in wood and fold,
Do fear and take us for very men:
Could the whip-poor-will or the cat of the glen
    Look into my eyes and be bold?

I am black, I am black!
　　But, once, I laughed in girlish glee,
For one of my colour stood in the track
　　Where the drivers drove, and looked at me,
And tender and full was the look he gave –
Could a slave look *so* at another slave? –
　　I look at the sky and the sea.

And from that hour our spirits grew
　　As free as if unsold, unbought:
Oh, strong enough, since we were two,
　　To conquer the world, we thought.
The drivers drove us day by day;
We did not mind, we went one way,
　　And no better a freedom sought.

In the sunny ground between the canes,
　　He said 'I love you' as he passed;
When the shingle-roof rang sharp with the rains,
　　I heard how he vowed it fast:
While others shook he smiled in the hut,
As he carved me a bowl of the cocoa-nut
　　Through the roar of the hurricanes.

I sang his name instead of a song,
　　Over and over I sang his name,
Upward and downward I drew it along
　　My various notes, – the same, the same!
I sang it low, that the slave-girls near
Might never guess, from aught they could hear,
　　It was only a name – a name.

I look on the sky and the sea.
    We were two to love, and two to pray:
Yes, two, O God, who cried to Thee,
    Though nothing didst Thou say!
Coldly Thou sat'st behind the sun:
And now I cry who am but one,
    Thou wilt not speak to-day.

We were black, we were black,
    We had no claim to love and bliss,
What marvel if each went to wrack?
    They wrung my cold hands out of his,
They dragged him – where? I crawled to touch
His blood's mark in the dust . . . not much.
    Ye pilgrim-souls, though plain as *this!*

Wrong, followed by a deeper wrong!
    Mere grief's too good for such as I:
So the white men brought the shame ere long
    To strangle the sob of my agony.
They would not leave me for my dull
Wet eyes! – it was too merciful
    To let me weep pure tears and die.

I am black, I am black!
    I wore a child upon my breast,
An amulet that hung too slack,
    And, in my unrest, could not rest:
Thus we went moaning, child and mother,
One to another, one to another,
    Until all ended for the best.

For hark! I will tell you low, low,
     I am black, you see, –
And the babe who lay on my bosom so,
     Was far too white, too white for me;
As white as the ladies who scorned to pray
Beside me at church but yesterday,
     Thou my tears had washed a place for my knee.

My own, own child! I could not bear
     To look in his face, it was so white;
I covered him up with a kerchief there,
     I covered his face in close and tight:
And he moaned and struggled, as well might be,
For the white child wanted his liberty –
     Ha, ha! he wanted the master-right.

He moaned and beat with his head and feet,
     His little feet that never grew;
He struck them out, as it was meet,
     Against my heart to break it through:
I might have sung and made him mild,
But I dared not sing to the white-faced child
     The only song I knew.

I pulled the kerchief very close:
     He could not see the sun, I swear,
More, then, alive, than now he does
     From between the roots of the mango ... where?
I know where. Close! A child and mother
Do wrong to look at one another
     When one is black and one is fair.

Why, in that single glance I had
    Of my child's face, . . . I tell you all,
I saw a look that made me mad!
    The *master's* look, that used to fall
On my soul like his lash . . . or worse!
And so, to save it from my curse,
    I twisted it round in my shawl.

And he moaned and trembled from foot to head,
    He shivered from head to foot;
Till after a time, he lay instead
    Too suddenly still and mute.
I felt, beside, a stiffening cold:
I dared to lift up just a fold,
    As in lifting a leaf of the mango-fruit.

But *my* fruit . . . ha, ha! – there, had been
    (I laugh to think on't at this hour!)
Your fine white angels (who have seen
    Nearest the secret of God's power)
And plucked my fruit to make them wine,
And sucked the soul of that child of mine
    As the humming-bird sucks the soul of the flower.

Ha, ha, the trick of the angel's white!
    They freed the white child's spirit so.
I said not a word, but day and night
    I carried the body to and fro,
And it lay on my heart like a stone, as chill.
– The sun may shine out as much as he will:
    I am cold, though it happened a month ago.

From the white man's house, and the black man's hut,
  I carried the little body on;
The forest's arms did round us shut,
  And silence through the trees did run:
They asked no question as I went,
They stood too high for astonishment,
  They could see God sit on His throne.

My little body, kerchiefed fast,
  I bore it on through the forest, on;
And when I felt it was tired at last,
  I scooped a hole beneath the moon:
Through the forest-tops the angels far,
With a white sharp finger from every star,
  Did point and mock at what was done.

Yet when it was all done aright, –
  Earth, 'twixt me and my baby, strewed, –
All, changed to black earth, – nothing white, –
  A dark child in the dark! – ensued
Some comfort, and my heart grew young;
I sate down smiling there and sung
  The song I learnt in my maidenhood.

And thus we two were reconciled,
  The white child and black mother, thus;
For as I sang it soft and wild,
  The same song, more melodious,
Rose from the grave whereon I sate:
It was the dead child singing that,
  To join the souls of both of us.

I look on the sea and the sky.
    Where the pilgrims' ships first anchored lay
The free sun rideth gloriously,
    But the pilgrim-ghosts have slid away
Through the earliest streaks of the morn:
My face is black, but it glares with a scorn
    Which they dare not meet by day.

Ha! – in their stead, their hunter sons!
    Ha, ha! they are on me – they hunt in a ring!
Keep off! I brave you all at once,
    I throw off your eyes like snakes that sting!
You have killed the black eagle at nest, I think:
Did you ever stand still in your triumph, and shrink
    From the stroke of her wounded wing?

(Man, drop that stone you dared to lift! –)
    I wish you who stand there five abreast,
Each, for his own wife's joy and gift,
    A little corpse as safely at rest
As mine in the mangoes! Yes, but *she*
May keep live babies on her knee,
    And sing the song she likes the best.

I am not mad: I am black.
    I see you staring in my face –
I know you staring, shrinking back,
    Ye are born of the Washington-race,
And this land is the free America,
And this mark on my wrist – (I prove what I say)
    Ropes tied me up here to the flogging-place.

You think I shrieked then? Not a sound!
    I hung, as a gourd hangs in the sun;
I only cursed them all around
    As softly as I might have done
My very own child: from these sands
Up to the mountains, lift your hands,
    O slaves, and end what I begun!

Whips, curses; these must answer those!
    For in this UNION you have set
Two kinds of men in adverse rows,
    Each loathing each; and all forget
The seven wounds in Christ's body fair,
While HE sees gaping everywhere
    Our countless wounds that pay no debt.

Our wounds are different. Your white men
    Are, after all, not gods indeed,
Nor able to make Christs again
    Do good with bleeding. We who bleed
(Stand off!) we help not in our loss!
We are too heavy for our cross,
    And fall and crush you and your seed.

I fall, I swoon! I look at the sky.
    The clouds are breaking on my brain;
I am floated along, as if I should die
    Of liberty's exquisite pain.
In the name of the white child waiting for me
In the death-dark where we may kiss and agree,
White men, I leave you all curse-free
    In my broken heart's disdain!

Consolation

All are not taken; there are left behind
Living Beloveds, tender looks to bring
And make the daylight still a happy thing,
And tender voices, to make soft the wind:
But if it were not so – if I could find
No love in all the world for comforting,
Nor any path but hollowly did ring
Where 'dust to dust' the love from life disjoined,
And if, before those sepulchres unmoving
I stood alone, (as some forsaken lamb
Goes bleating up the moors in weary dearth,)
Crying 'Where are ye, O my loved and loving?' –
I know a Voice would sound, 'Daughter, I AM.
Can I suffice for HEAVEN and not for earth?'

Memory and Hope

Back-looking Memory
And prophet Hope both sprang from out the ground;
One, where the flashing of cherubic sword
        Fell sad in Eden's ward,
And one, from Eden earth within the sound
Of the four rivers lapsing pleasantly,
What time the promise after curse was said,
        'Thy seed shall bruise his head.'

Poor Memory's brain is wild,
As moonstruck by that flaming atmosphere
When she was born; her deep eyes shine and shone
        With light that conquereth sun
And stars to wanner paleness year by year:
With odorous gums she mixeth things defiled,
She trampleth down earth's grasses green and sweet
        With her far-wandering feet.

She plucketh many flowers,
Their beauty on her bosom's coldness killing;
She teacheth every melancholy sound
    To winds and waters round;
She droppeth tears with seed where man is tilling
The rugged soil in his exhausted hours;
She smileth – ah me! in her smile doth go
    A mood of deeper woe.

Hope tripped on out of sight,
Crowned with an Eden wreath she saw not wither,
And went a-nodding through the wilderness
    With brow that shone no less
Than a sea-gull's wing, brought nearer by rough weather,
Searching the treeless rock for fruits of light;
Her fair quick feet being armed from stones and cold
    By slippers of pure gold.

Memory did Hope much wrong
And, while she dreamed, her slippers stole away;
But still she wended on with mirth unheeding,
    Although her feet were bleeding,
Till Memory tracked her on a certain day,
And with most evil eyes did search her long
And cruelly, whereat she sank to ground
    In a stark deadly swound.

And so my Hope were slain,
Had it not been that THOU wast standing near
Oh Thou who saidest 'live,' to creatures lying
    In their own blood and dying!
For Thou her forehead to Thine heart didst rear
And make its silent pulses sing again,
Pouring a new light o'er her darkened eyne
    With tender tears from Thine.

Therefore my Hope arose
From out her swound and gazed upon Thy face,
And, meeting there that soft subduing look
    Which Peter's spirit shook,
Sank downward in a rapture to embrace
Thy piercëd hands and feet with kisses close,
And prayed Thee to assist her evermore
    To 'reach the things before.'

Then gavest Thou the smile
Whence angel-wings thrill quick like summer lightning,
Vouchsafing rest beside Thee, where she never
    From Love and Faith may sever:-
Whereat the Eden crown she saw not whitening
A time ago, though whitening all the while,
Reddened with life to hear the Voice which talked
    To Adam as he walked.

Human Life's Mystery

We sow the glebe, we reap the corn,
    We build the house where we may rest,
And then, at moments, suddenly
We look up to the great wide sky,
Inquiring wherefore we were born,
    For earnest or for jest?

The senses folding thick and dark
    About the stifled soul within,
We guess diviner things beyond,
And yearn to them with yearning fond;
We strike out blindly to a mark
    Believed in, but not seen.

We vibrate to the pant and thrill
　Wherewith Eternity has curled
In serpent-twine about God's seat:
While, freshening upward to His feet,
In gradual growth His full-leaved will
　Expands from world to world.

And, in the tumult and excess
　Of act and passion under sun,
We sometimes hear – oh, soft and far,
As silver star did touch with star,
The kiss of Peace and Righteousness
　Through all things that are done.

God keeps His holy mysteries
　Just on the outside of man's dream;
In diapason slow, we think
To hear their pinions rise and sink,
While they float pure beneath His eyes,
　Like swans adown a stream.

Abstractions, are they, from the forms
　Of His great beauty? – exaltations
From His great glory? – strong previsions
Of what we shall be? – intuitions
Of what we are – in calms and storms
　Beyond our peace and passions?

Things nameless! which, in passing so,
　Do stroke us with a subtle grace;
We say, 'Who passes?' – they are dumb;
We cannot see them go or come,
Their touches fall soft, cold, as snow
　Upon a blind man's face.

Yet, touching so they draw above
   Our common thoughts to Heaven's unknown;
Our daily joy and pain advance
To a divine significance,
Our human love – O mortal love,
   That light is not its own!

And sometimes horror chills our blood
   To be so near such mystic Things,
And we wrap round us for defence
Our purple manners, moods of sense –
As angels from the face of God
   Stand hidden in their wings.

And sometimes through life's heavy swound
   We grope for them, with strangled breath
We stretch our hands abroad and try
To reach them in our agony;
And widen, so, the broad life-wound
   Soon large enough for death.

Sleeping and Watching

Sleep on, baby, on the floor,
   Tired of all the playing:
Sleep with smile the sweeter for
   That, you dropped away in.
On your curls' full roundness stand
   Golden lights serenely;
One cheek, pushed out by the hand,
   Folds the dimple inly:
Little head and little foot
   Heavy laid for pleasure,
Underneath the lids half shut,
   Slants the shining azure.
Open-soul in noonday sun,

So you lie and slumber:
Nothing evil having done,
Nothing can encumber.

I, who cannot sleep as well,
  Shall I sigh to view you?
Or sigh further to foretell
  All that may undo you?
Nay, keep smiling, little child,
  Ere the sorrow neareth:
I will smile too! patience mild
  Pleasure's token weareth.
Nay, keep sleeping before loss:
  I shall sleep though losing!
As by cradle, so by cross,
  Sure is the reposing.

And God knows who sees us twain,
  Child at childish leisure,
I am near as tired of pain
  As you seem of pleasure.
Very soon too, by His grace
  Gently wrapt around me,
Shall I show as calm a face,
  Shall I sleep as soundly.
Differing in this, that you
  Clasp your playthings, sleeping,
While my hand shall drop the few
  Given to my keeping:
Differing in this, that I
  Sleeping shall be colder,
And in waking presently,
  Brighter to beholder:
Differing in this beside
  (Sleeper, have you heard me?
Do you move, and open wide
  Eyes of wonder toward me?)

That while you I thus recall
From your sleep, I solely,
Me from mine an angel shall,
With reveillie holy.

The Soul's Expression

With stammering lips and insufficient sound
I strive and struggle to deliver right
That music of my nature, day and night
With dream and thought and feeling interwound,
And inly answering all the senses round
With octaves of a mystic depth and height
Which step out grandly to the infinite
From the dark edges of the sensual ground.
This song of soul I struggle to outbear
Through portals of the sense, sublime and whole,
And utter all myself into the air:
But if I did it – as the thunder-roll
Breaks its own cloud, my flesh would perish there,
Before that dread apocalypse of soul.

Life

Each creature holds an insular point in space;
Yet what man stirs a finger, breathes a sound,
But all the multitudinous beings round
In all the countless worlds with time and place
For their conditions, down to the central base,
Thrill, haply, in vibration and rebound,
Life answering life across the vast profound,
In full antiphony, by a common grace?
I think this sudden joyaunce which illumes
A child's mouth sleeping, unaware may run
From some soul newly loosened from earth's tombs:

I think this passionate sigh, which half-begun
I stifle back, may reach and stir the plumes
Of God's calm angel standing in the sun.

Bereavement

When some Belovèds, 'neath whose eyelids lay
The sweet lights of my childhood, one by one
Did leave me dark before the natural sun,
And I astonied fell and could not pray –
A thought within me to myself did say,
'Is God less God, that *thou* art left undone?
Rise, worship, bless Him, in this sackcloth spun,
As in that purple!' – But I answered, Nay!
What child his filial heart in words can loose
If he behold his tender father raise
The hand that chastens sorely? can he choose
But sob in silence with an upward gaze? –
And *my* great Father, thinking fit to bruise,
Discerns in speechless tears both prayer and praise.

Grief

I tell you, hopeless grief is passionless;
That only men incredulous of despair,
    Half-taught in anguish, through the midnight air
Beat upward to God's throne in loud access
Of shrieking and reproach. Full desertness
    In souls as countries lieth silent-bare
    Under the blanching, vertical eye-glare
Of the absolute Heavens. Deep-hearted man, express
Grief for thy Dead in silence like to Death –
    Most like a monumental statue set
In everlasting watch and moveless woe

Till itself crumble to the dust beneath.
Touch it; the marble eyelids are not wet:
If it could weep, it could arise and go.

HARRIET BEECHER STOWE
1811–1896

Harriet Beecher Stowe was the daughter of a stern Calvinist, Lyman
Beecher. He was a vigorous man, who worked off surplus energy by
shovelling piles of sand from one side to the other of his cellar. He also
played the violin and the piano. Harriet's mother Roxana died when
Harriet was only four, after giving birth to eight children. She wanted
all her sons to become ministers, a wish that was fulfilled by all but one
of Harriet's six brothers.

Harriet had several black friends, particularly her mother's washer-
woman, Candace, who was devoted to the memory of her dead mistress.
Dinah, her aunt's servant, was another who left a strong impression on
little Harriet. She preferred these kindly women to the imposing new
Mrs Beecher, whom the children found fine and elegant – and
frightening.

Harriet's education was two-thirds religious. She was troubled by
religious doubts of some kind all her life, but her passionate belief in
causes made up for that. She had seven children, one of whom died of
cholera. In the midst of rearing her family she became caught up in the
abolitionist movement, of which her father's seminary was a hot-bed.
She wrote *Uncle Tom's Cabin, or Life among the Lowly*, after finishing
nursing her seventh child. Ten thousand copies were sold in a week.
The sales went up to 300,000 in the space of a year. Because the rights
were not assured, and foreign editions were all pirated, she did not
make out of it the fortune that she should have done, but it did
nevertheless change the family fortunes from abject poverty to
comfort. Meanwhile she became loathed in the south. A cousin in

Georgia could receive no letter from her if her name was on the outside! Her second venture into controversy was an attack on Byron about his affair with his sister, Mrs Leigh. This made her name anathema in British circles where she had hitherto been welcomed. All in all, she was brave, conscientious and kind, though often misguided in the nature of her campaigning, not realising how her words would touch others. But she was incorruptible. Fame changed her not at all. She never learned to manage money, and ended her days in a dreamy state, thinking the gold medal she was brought was merely a toy. Yet she was a deeply religious, sincere woman whose works had a profound effect, particularly on the anti-slavery movement. Her religious poetry is patchy, but well worth reading, for in it she captures the pathos that was keynote to her fiction, and reveals the sincerity that was her hallmark.

Mary at the Cross

'Now there stood by the cross of Jesus his Mother.'

O wondrous Mother! since the dawn of time
Was ever love, was ever grief, like thine?
O highly favored in thy joy's deep flow,
And favored even in this, thy bitterest woe!

Poor was that home in simple Nazareth
    Where, fairly growing, like some silent flower,
Last of a kingly race, unknown and lowly,
    O desert lily, passed thy childhood's hour.

The world knew not the tender, serious maiden,
    Who through deep loving years so silent grew,
Full of high thought and holy aspiration,
    Which the o'ershadowing God alone might view.

And then it came, that message from the highest,
Such as to woman ne'er before descended,
The Almighty wings thy prayerful soul o'erspread,
And with thy life the Life of worlds was blended.

What visions then of future glory filled thee,
The chosen mother of the King unknown,
Mother fulfiller of all prophecy
Which through dim ages wondering seers had shown!

Well did thy dark eye kindle, thy deep soul
Rise into billows, and thy heart rejoice;
Then woke the poet's fire, the prophet's song,
Tuned with strange burning words thy timid voice.

Then, in dark contrast, came the lowly manger,
The outcast shed, the tramp of brutal feet;
Again behold earth's learned and her lowly,
Sages and shepherds prostrate at thy feet.

Then to the temple bearing, hark again
What strange conflicting tones of prophecy
Breathe o'er the child, foreshadowing words of joy,
High triumph blent with bitter agony!

O, highly favored thou in many an hour
Spent in lone musings with thy wondrous Son!
When thou didst gaze into that glorious eye,
And hold that mighty hand within thine own.

Blest through those thirty years, when in thy dwelling
He lived a God disguised with unknown power;
And thou his sole adorer, his best love,
Trusting, revering, waited for his hour.

Blest in that hour when called by opening heaven
  With cloud and voice, and the baptizing flame,
Up from the Jordan walked the acknowledged stranger,
  And awestruck crowds grew silent as he came.

Blessed, when full of grace, with glory crowned,
  He from both hands almighty favors poured,
And though He had not where to lay his head,
  Brought to his feet alike the slave and lord.

Crowds followed; thousands shouted, 'Lo, our King!'
  Fast beat thy heart. Now, now the hour draws nigh:
Behold the crown, the throne, the nations bend!
  Ah, no! fond mother, no! behold him die!

Now by that cross thou tak'st thy final station,
  And shar'st the last dark trial of thy Son;
Not with weak tears or woman's lamentation,
  But with high silent anguish like his own.

Hail! highly favored, even in this deep passion;
  Hail! in this bitter anguish thou art blest, –
Blest in the holy power with him to suffer
  Those deep death-pangs that lead to higher rest.

All now is darkness; and in that deep stillness
  The God-man wrestles with that mighty woe;
Hark to that cry, the rock of ages rending, –
  ''Tis finished!' Mother, all is glory now!

By sufferings mighty as his mighty soul,
  Hath the Redeemer risen forever blest;
And through all ages must his heart-beloved
  Through the same baptism enter the same rest.

Hours of the Night

SIMON THE CYRENIAN

'They laid hold upon one Simon a Cyrenian, and on him they laid the
cross, that he might bear it after Jesus.'

Along the dusty thoroughfare of life,
  Upon his daily errands walking free,
Came a brave, honest man, untouched by pain,
  Unchilled by sight or thought of misery.

But lo! a crowd: – he stops – with curious eye
  A fainting form all pressed to earth he sees;
The hard, rough burden of the bitter cross
  Hath bowed the drooping head and feeble knees.

Ho! lay the cross upon yon stranger there,
  For he hath breadth of chest and strength of limb!
Straight it is done; and heavy-laden thus,
  With Jesus' cross, he turns and follows him.

Unmurmuring, patient, cheerful, pitiful,
  Prompt with the holy sufferer to endure,
Forsaking all to follow the dear Lord, –
  Thus did he make his glorious calling sure.

O soul, whoe'er thou art, walking life's way,
  As yet from touch of deadly sorrow free,
Learn from this story to forecast the day
  When Jesus and his cross shall come to thee.

O, in that fearful, that decisive hour,
  Rebel not, shrink not, seek not thence to flee,
But, humbly bending, take thy heavy load,
  And bear it after Jesus patiently.

His cross is thine. If thou and he be one,
  Some portion of his pain must still be thine;
Thus only may'st thou share his glorious crown,
  And reign with him in majesty divine.

Master in sorrow! I accept my share
  In the great anguish of life's mystery.
No more, alone, I sink beneath my load,
  But bear my cross, O Jesus, after thee.

CHARLOTTE BRONTË
1816–1855

Charlotte Brontë was born at Thornton in the parish of Bradford in 1816. She was the third child of the Reverend Patrick Brontë, an Irishman, and his Cornish wife, Maria, and her younger siblings were Branwell, Emily and Anne.

Patrick Brontë was a difficult, quick-tempered, intelligent man who did all he could to promote his children's intellectual development. But he could not afford a really good education for them, nor do much beyond feeding them once they grew up. As a result the girls were sent to the Clergy Daughters' School at Cowan Bridge, which is depicted in such appalling terms as Lowood in *Jane Eyre*. After their two elder sisters died of TB contracted there, Charlotte and Emily returned home and continued their education privately. Their lives were quite circumscribed. There was little social contact, but there were lots of opportunities for writing stories and playing the extraordinary imaginary games recorded in the early Brontë works, such as *Tales from Angria*. They all grew to love the moors around their home. But in 1831, Charlotte was sent to Miss Wooler's school at Roe Head, which was a success as far as she was concerned, a far cry from Cowan Bridge. There she made friends with Ellen Nussey, to whom she remained close all her life. In 1835 she returned to Miss Wooler's school as a teacher and stayed for three years.

She refused two offers of marriage, including one from Ellen Nussey's brother, which meant she had to earn her own living. She worked as a governess, in true Victorian style, and found her first position intolerable but the second acceptable, if not joyful. In 1840–41 the sisters decided to start their own school for girls. Although that never came about, it led to Charlotte and Emily going off to Brussels to learn French. They stayed until their Aunt Elizabeth's death in the autumn of 1842, and Charlotte returned there alone in the spring of 1843, where she fell passionately in love with Monsieur Héger, one of the couple who ran the *pensionnat* where they had been staying. Both *The Professor* and *Villette* demonstrate the importance of her experiences in Brussels in her life.

In 1845 the three sisters began to write furiously. They had a volume of poems published, under the pseudonyms of Currer, Ellis and Acton Bell, in 1846. It went unnoticed, but Emily's *Wuthering Heights* was accepted that year, as was Anne's *Agnes Grey*. Charlotte's *The Professor* was turned down (it was only published after her death), but *Jane Eyre*, which she began in 1846, was published in 1847 and made her name with its instant success.

By January 1848 *Jane Eyre* was in its second edition, but at the same time Branwell was destroying himself with drink and drugs, Emily contracted TB and Anne developed it too. Branwell died in September, Emily in December and Anne in early 1849. Charlotte remained in Haworth, writing first *Shirley* and then *Villette*, and making frequent trips to London, Scotland and Manchester, where she met Mrs Gaskell, who was to have a profound influence on her and was later to write her biography.

In 1854 Charlotte married her father's curate, Mr Nicholls, but it was too late. Throughout her life she had been diffident and had felt inferior. She entered married life without enthusiasm, and died, pregnant, in March 1855. Success never cured her of her low self-esteem, and her life, though outwardly successful, held much tragedy and probably considerable dissatisfaction. Those emotions combine to form a sense of spiritual awareness, and some impatience with religion. Charlotte's poetry has never been thought very distinguished. What it has, however, is a lightness of touch and a self-conscious awareness of her own beliefs. It is well worth reading.

'I now had only to retrace'

I now had only to retrace
The long and lonely road
So lately in the rainbow chase
With fearless ardour trod.

Behind I left the sunshine now
The evening setting sun,
Before a storm rolled dark and low
Some gloomy hills upon.

It came with rain – it came with wind,
With swollen stream it howled,
And night advancing black and blind
In ebon horror scowled.

Lost in the hills – all painfully
I climbed a heathy peak.
I sought I longed afar to see
My life's light's parting streak.

The West was black as if no day
Had ever lingered there,
As if no red expiring ray
Had tinged the enkindled air.

And morning's portals could not lie
Where yon dark Orient spread.
The funeral North – the black dark sky
Alike mourned [   ] dead.

'Turn not now for comfort here'

Turn not now for comfort here;
  The lamps are quenched, the moors are gone;
Cold and lonely, dim and drear,
  Void are now those hills of stone.

Sadly sighing, Anvale woods
  Whisper peace to my decay;
Fir-tree over pine-tree broods
  Dark and high and piled away.

Gone are all who saw my glory
  Fill on festal nights the trees
Distant lit, now silver hoary,
  Bowed they to the freshening breeze.

They are dead who heard at night
  Woods and winds and waters sound,
Where my casements cast their light
  Red upon the snow-piled ground.

Some from afar in foreign regions,
  Some from drear suffering – wild unrest,
All light on land and winged legions
  Fill the old woods and parent nest.

The Teacher's Monologue

The room is quiet, thoughts alone
  People its mute tranquillity;
The yoke put off, the long task done –
  I am, as it is bliss to be,
Still and untroubled. Now, I see,
  For the first time, how soft the day
O'er waveless water, stirless tree,

Silent and sunny, wings its way.
Now, as I watch that distant hill,
   So faint, so blue, so far removed,
Sweet dreams of home my heart may fill,
   That home where I am known and loved:
It lies beyond; yon azure brow
   Parts me from all Earth holds for me;
And, morn and eve, my yearnings flow
   Thitherward tending, changelessly.
My happiest hours, ay! all the time,
   I love to keep in memory,
Lapsed among moors, ere life's first prime
   Decayed to dark anxiety.

Sometimes, I think a narrow heart
   Makes me thus mourn those far away,
And keeps my love so far apart
   From friends and friendships of to-day;
Sometimes, I think 'tis but a dream
   I treasure up so jealously,
All the sweet thoughts I live on seem
   To vanish into vacancy:
And then, this strange, coarse world around
   Seems all that's palpable and true;
And every sight and every sound
   Combines my spirit to subdue
To aching grief; so void and lone
   Is Life and Earth – so worse than vain,
The hopes that, in my own heart sown,
   And cherished by such sun and rain
As Joy and transient Sorrow shed,
   Have ripened to a harvest there:
Alas! methinks I hear it said,
   'Thy golden sheaves are empty air.'
All fades away; my very home
   I think will soon be desolate;
I hear, at times, a warning come

Of bitter partings at its gate;
And, if I should return and see
   The hearth-fire quenched, the vacant chair;
And hear it whispered mournfully,
   That farewells have been spoken there,
What shall I do, and whither turn?
Where look for peace? When cease to mourn?

*

'Tis not the air I wished to play,
   The strain I wished to sing;
My wilful spirit slipped away
   And struck another string.
I neither wanted smile nor tear,
   Bright joy nor bitter woe,
But just a song that sweet and clear,
   Though haply sad, might flow.

A quiet song, to solace me
   When sleep refused to come;
A strain to chase despondency
   When sorrowful for home.
In vain I try; I cannot sing;
   All feels so cold and dead
No wild distress, no gushing spring
   Of tears in anguish shed;

But all the impatient gloom of one
   Who waits a distant day,
When, some great task of suffering done,
   Repose shall toil repay.
For youth departs, and pleasure flies,
   And life consumes away,
And youth's rejoicing ardour dies
   Beneath this drear delay;

And Patience, weary with her yoke,
  Is yielding to despair,
And Health's elastic spring is broke
  Beneath the strain of care.
Life will be gone ere I have lived;
  Where now is Life's first prime?
I've worked and studied, longed and grieved,
  Through all that rosy time.

To toil, to think, to long, to grieve –
  Is such my future fate?
The morn was dreary, must the eve
  Be also desolate?
Well, such a life at least makes Death
  A welcome, wished-for friend;
Then, aid me, Reason, Patience, Faith,
  To suffer to the end!

The Missionary

Plough, vessel, plough the British main,
Seek the free ocean's wider plain;
Leave English scenes and English skies,
Unbind, dissever English ties;
Bear me to climes remote and strange,
Where altered life, fast-following change,
Hot action, never-ceasing toil,
Shall stir, turn, dig, the spirit's soil;
Fresh roots shall plant, fresh seed shall sow,
Till a new garden there shall grow,
Cleared of the weeds that fill it now –
Mere human love, mere selfish yearning,
Which, cherished, would arrest me yet.
I grasp the plough, there's no returning,
Let me, then, struggle to forget.

But England's shores are yet in view,
And England's skies of tender blue
Are arched above her guardian sea.
I cannot yet Remembrance flee;
I must again, then, firmly face
That task of anguish, to retrace,
Wedded to home – I home forsake;
Fearful of change – I changes make;
Too fond of ease – I plunge in toil;
Lover of calm – I seek turmoil:
Nature and hostile Destiny
Stir in my heart a conflict wild;
And long and fierce the war will be
Ere duty both has reconciled.

What other tie yet holds me fast
To the divorced, abandoned past?
Smouldering, on my heart's altar lies
The fire of some great sacrifice,
Not yet half quenched. The sacred steel
But lately struck my carnal will,
My life-long hope, first joy and last,
What I loved well, and clung to fast;
What I wished wildly to retain,
What I renounced with soul-felt pain;
What – when I saw it, axe-struck, perish –
Left me no joy on earth to cherish;
A man bereft – yet sternly now
I do confirm that Jephtha vow:
Shall I retract, or fear, or flee?
Did Christ, when rose the fatal tree
Before Him, on Mount Calvary?
'Twas a long fight, hard fought, but won,
And what I did was justly done.

Yet, Helen! from thy love I turned,
When my heart most for thy heart burned;
I dared thy tears, I dared thy scorn –
Easier the death-pang had been borne.
Helen, thou might'st not go with me,
I could not – dared not stay for thee!
I heard afar, in bonds complain
The savage from beyond the main;
And that wild sound rose o'er the cry
Wrung out by passion's agony;
And even when, with the bitterest tear
I ever shed, mine eyes were dim,
Still, with the spirit's vision clear,
I saw Hell's empire, vast and grim,
Spread on each Indian river's shore,
Each realm of Asia covering o'er.
There the weak, trampled by the strong,
Live but to suffer – hopeless die;
There pagan-priests, whose creed is Wrong,
Extortion, Lust and Cruelty,
Crush our lost race – and brimming fill
The bitter cup of human ill;
And I – who have the healing creed,
The faith benign of Mary's Son,
Shall I behold my brother's need,
And selfishly to aid him shun?
I who upon my mother's knees,
In childhood, read Christ's written word,
Received His legacy of peace,
His holy rule of action heard;
I – in whose heart the sacred sense
Of Jesus' love was early felt;
Of His pure, full benevolence,
His pitying tenderness for guilt;
His shepherd-care for wandering sheep,
For all weak, sorrowing, trembling things,
His mercy vast, His passion deep

Of anguish for man's sufferings;
I – schooled from childhood in such lore –
Dared I draw back or hesitate,
When called to heal the sickness sore
Of those far off and desolate?
Dark, in the realm and shades of Death,
Nations, and tribes, and empires lie,
But even to them the light of Faith
Is breaking on their sombre sky:
And be it mine to bid them raise
Their drooped heads to the kindling scene,
And know and hail the sunrise blaze
Which heralds Christ the Nazarene.
I know how Hell the veil will spread
Over their brows and filmy eyes,
And earthward crush the lifted head
That would look up and seek the skies;
I know what war the fiend will wage
Against that soldier of the Cross,
Who comes to dare his demon – rage,
And work his kingdom shame and loss.
Yes, hard and terrible the toil
Of him who steps on foreign soil,
Resolved to plant the gospel vine,
Where tyrants rule and slaves repine;
Eager to life Religion's light
Where thickest shades of mental night
Screen the false god and fiendish rite;
Reckless that missionary blood,
Shed in wild wilderness and wood,
Has left, upon the unblest air,
The man's deep moan – the martyr's prayer.
I know my lot – I only ask
Power to fulfil the glorious task;
Willing the spirit, may the flesh
Strength for the day receive afresh.

May burning sun or deadly wind
Prevail not o'er an earnest mind;
May torments strange or direst death
Nor trample truth, nor baffle faith.

Though such blood-drops should fall from me
As fell in old Gethsemane,
Welcome the anguish, so it gave
More strength to work – more skill to save.
And, oh! if brief must be my time,
If hostile hand or fatal clime
Cut short my course – still o'er my grave,
Lord, may Thy harvest whitening wave.
So I the culture may begin,
Let others thrust the sickle in;
If but the seed will faster grow,
May my blood water what I sow!
What! have I ever trembling stood,
And feared to give to God that blood?
What! has the coward love of life
Made me shrink from the righteous strife?
Have human passions, human fears
Severed me from those Pioneers
Whose task is to march first, and trace
Paths for the progress of our race?
It has been so; but grant me, Lord,
Now to stand steadfast by Thy word!
Protected by salvation's helm,
Shielded by faith, with truth begirt,
To smile when trials seek to whelm
And stand 'mid testing fires unhurt
Hurling Hell's strongest bulwarks down,
Even when the last pang thrills my breast,
When Death bestows the Martyr's crown,
And calls me into Jesus' rest.
Then for my ultimate reward –

Then for the world-rejoicing word –
The voice from Father – Spirit – Son:
'Servant of God, well hast thou done!'

On the Death of Anne Brontë

There's little joy in life for me,
    And little terror in the grave;
I've lived the parting hour to see
    Of one I would have died to save.

Calmly to watch the failing breath,
    Wishing each sigh might be the last;
Longing to see the shade of death
    O'er those beloved features cast.

The cloud, the stillness that must part
    The darling of my life from me;
And then to thank God from my heart,
    To thank Him well and fervently;

Although I knew that we had lost
    The hope and glory of our life;
And now, benighted, tempest-tossed,
    Must bear alone the weary strife.

On the Death of Emily Jane Brontë

My darling, thou wilt never know
The grinding agony of woe
    That we have borne for thee.
Thus may we consolation tear
E'en from the depth of our despair
    And wasting misery.

The nightly anguish thou art spared
When all the crushing truth is bared
    To the awakening mind,
When the galled heart is pierced with grief,
Till wildly it implores relief,
    But small relief can find.

Nor know'st thou what it is to lie
Looking forth with streaming eye
    On life's lone wilderness.
'Weary, weary, dark and drear,
How shall I the journey bear,
    The burden and distress?'

Then since thou art spared such pain
We will not wish thee here again;
    He that lives must mourn.
God help us through our misery
And give us rest and joy with thee
    When we reach our bourne!

EMILY BRONTË
1818–1848

Like her sisters, Emily Brontë was brought up at Haworth parsonage
on the bleak Yorkshire moors which she loved dearly, as is clear from
her poetry. Her sister Charlotte describes those moors as 'dark with
heath, shut in little valleys, where a stream waters, here and there, a
fringe of stunted copse. Mills and scattered cottages chase romance from
these valleys; it is only higher up, deep in amongst the ridges of the
moors, that Imagination can find rest for the sole of her foot: and even
if she finds it there, she must be a solitude-loving raven – no gentle dove.
If she demand beauty to inspire her, she must bring it inborn: these

moors are too stern to yield any product so delicate.' Yet in Emily's eyes
they were beautiful; perhaps she brought a beauty inborn.

Emily went to school briefly at the unspeakable Cowan Bridge, and
also went to Roe Head. In both cases, the experiences were unhappy,
more because of her inability to tolerate being away from home and the
moors than because of any cruelty inflicted upon her. Charlotte writes
that 'Liberty was the breath of Emily's nostrils; without it, she
perished.' Her response to school was to sicken and waste, which led to
her return home, and it was only much later that she risked absence
again, this time going abroad with Charlotte. In 1842 the two sisters
went to Brussels to study, but Emily did not like it and returned to
Yorkshire before the end of the year.

Back at Haworth, she lived a secluded, isolated life in which she
produced her best work, including many of the poems featured here.
Most of these, along with poems by Charlotte and Anne, were
published pseudonymously in 1846, two years before Emily's death
from the family disease, tuberculosis. Her novel *Wuthering Heights*
was published in 1847 and is still read with delight by many teenage
girls. Film sequences of Heathcliff and Cathy against the bleakness of
the moors have ensured Emily a lasting place in the popular
imagination.

But although *Wuthering Heights* is a fine, passionate and romantic
novel, the poems are in a different literary league. Unlike her sisters,
Emily Brontë ranks amongst the great English poets. Her imagination
is considerable, but it is her crafting of finely observed natural beauty on
to passionate verse which is so remarkable. Her death was a brave one,
as her last poem, 'No coward soul is mine', reveals. Of it Matthew
Arnold, a staunch admirer, wrote:

> (How shall I sing her?) whose soul
> Knew no fellow for might,
> Passion, vehemence, grief,
> Daring, since Byron died,
> That world-famed son of fire – she, who sank
> Baffled, unknown, self-consumed;
> Whose too-bold dying song
> Stirred, like a clarion-blast, my soul.

Stanzas
(perhaps by Emily Brontë)

Often rebuked, yet always back returning
    To those first feelings that were born with me,
And leaving busy chase of wealth and learning
    For idle dreams of things which cannot be:

To-day, I will seek not the shadowy region;
    Its unsustaining vastness waxes drear;
And visions rising, legion after legion,
    Bring the unreal world too strangely near.

I'll walk, but not in old heroic traces,
    And not in paths of high morality,
And not among the half-distinguished faces,
    The clouded forms of long-past history.

I'll walk where my own nature would be leading:
    It vexes me to choose another guide:
Where the gray flocks in ferny glens are feeding;
    Where the wild wind blows on the mountain side.

What have those lonely mountains worth revealing?
    More glory and more grief than I can tell:
The earth that wakes *one* human heart to feeling
    Can centre both the worlds of Heaven and Hell

The Visionary
(Emily Brontë with Charlotte Brontë)

Silent is the house: all are laid asleep:
One alone looks out o'er the snow-wreaths deep,
Watching every cloud, dreading every breeze
That whirls the 'wildering drift, and bends the groaning trees.

Cheerful is the hearth, soft the matted floor;
Not one shivering gust creeps through pane or door;
The little lamp burns straight, its rays shoot strong and far:
I trim it well, to be the wanderer's guiding-star.

Frown, my haughty sire! chide, my angry dame!
Set your slaves to spy; threaten me with shame:
But neither sire nor dame, nor prying serf shall know
What angel nightly tracks that waste of frozen snow.

What I love shall come like visitant of air,
Safe in secret power from lurking human snare;
Who loves me, no word of mine shall e'er betray,
Though for faith unstained my life must forfeit pay.

Burn then, little lamp; glimmer straight and clear –
Hush! a rustling wing stirs, methinks, the air:
He for whom I wait thus ever comes to me;
Strange Power! I trust thy might; trust thou my constancy.

Faith and Despondency

'The winter wind is loud and wild:
Come close to me, my darling child;
Forsake thy books, and mateless play,
And, while the night is gathering grey,
We'll talk its pensive hours away.

'Ierně, round our sheltered hall
November's gusts unheeded call;
Not one faint breath can enter here
Enough to wave my daughter's hair;
And I am glad to watch the blaze
Glance from her eyes with mimic rays;
To feel her cheek so softly pressed,
In happy quiet on my breast.

'But, yet, even this tranquillity
Brings bitter, restless thoughts to me;
And, in the red fire's cheerful glow,
I think of deep glens, blocked with snow;
I dream of moor, and misty hill,
Where evening closes dark and chill;
For, lone, among the mountains cold
Lie those that I have loved of old.
And my heart aches, in hopeless pain,
Exhausted with repinings vain,
That I shall greet them ne'er again!'

'Father, in early infancy,
When you were far beyond the sea,
Such thoughts were tyrants over me!
I often sat, for hours together,
Through the long nights of angry weather,
Raised on my pillow, to descry
The dim moon struggling in the sky;
Or, with strained ear, to catch the shock,
Of rock with wave, and wave with rock;
So would I fearful vigil keep,
And, all for listening, never sleep.
But this world's life has much to dread:
Not so, my father, with the dead.

'Oh! not for them should we despair –
The grave is drear, but they are not there:
Their dust is mingled with the sod;
Their happy souls are gone to God!
You told me this, and yet you sigh,
And murmur that your friends must die.
Ah! my dear father, tell me why?
For, if your former words were true,
    How useless would such sorrow be!
As wise, to mourn the seed which grew
    Unnoticed on its parent tree,

Because it fell in fertile earth,
And sprang up to a glorious birth –
Struck deep its root, and lifted high
Its green boughs in the breezy sky.

'But I'll not fear: I will not weep
For those whose bodies rest in sleep –
I know there is a blessed shore,
    Opening its ports for me and mine;
And, gazing Time's wide waters o'er,
    I weary for that land divine,
Where we were born, where you and I
Shall meet our dearest, when we die;
From suffering and corruption free,
Restored into the Deity.'

'Well hast thou spoken, sweet, trustful child!
    And wiser than thy sire;
And worldly tempests, raging wild,
    Shall strengthen thy desire –
Thy fervent hope, through storm and foam,
    Through wind and ocean's roar,
To reach, at last, the eternal home,
    The steadfast, changeless shore!'

The Philosopher

Enough of thought, philosopher!
    Too long hast thou been dreaming
Unlightened in this chamber drear
    While summer's sun is beaming!
Space-sweeping soul, what sad refrain
    Concludes thy musings once again?
'Oh, for the time when I shall sleep
    Without identity,
And never care how rain may steep,

Or snow may cover me!
No promised heaven, these wild desires
    Could all, or half fulfil;
No threatened hell, with quenchless fires,
    Subdue this quenchless will!'

'So said I, and still say the same;
    Still, to my death, will say –
Three gods, within this little frame,
    Are warring, night and day;
Heaven could not hold them all, and yet
    They all are held in me;
And must be mine till I forget
    My present entity!
Oh, for the time, when in my breast
    Their struggles will be o'er!
Oh, for the day, when I shall rest,
    And never suffer more!'

'I saw a spirit, standing, man,
    Where thou dost stand – an hour ago,
And round his feet three rivers ran,
    Of equal depth, and equal flow –
A golden stream – and one like blood;
    And one like sapphire seemed to be;
But where they joined their triple flood
    It tumbled in an inky sea.
The spirit sent his dazzling gaze
    Down through that ocean's gloomy night;
Then, kindling all, with sudden blaze,
    The glad deep sparkled wide and bright –
White as the sun, far, far more fair
    Than its divided sources were!'

'And even for that spirit, seer,
    I've watched and sought my lifetime long;
Sought him in heaven, hell, earth, and air,

An endless search, and always wrong.
Had I but seen his glorious eye
    Once light the clouds that 'wilder me,
I ne'er had raised this coward cry
    To cease to think, and cease to be;
I ne'er had called oblivion blest,
    Nor, stretching eager hands to death,
Implored to change for senseless rest
    This sentient soul, this living breath.
Oh, let me die – that power and will
    Their cruel strife may close;
And conquered good and conquering ill
    Be lost in one repose!'

Death

Death! that struck when I was most confiding
    In my certain faith of joy to be –
Strike again, Time's withered branch dividing
    From the fresh root of Eternity!

Leaves, upon Time's branch, were growing brightly,
    Full of sap, and full of silver-dew;
Birds beneath its shelter gathered nightly;
    Daily round its flowers the wild bees flew.

Sorrow passed, and plucked the golden blossom;
    Guilt stripped off the foliage in its pride;
But, within its parent's kindly bosom,
    Flowed for ever Life's restoring tide.

Little mourned I for the parted gladness,
    For the vacant nest and silent song –
Hope was there, and laughed me out of sadness,
    Whispering, 'Winter will not linger long!'

And, behold! with tenfold increase blessing,
   Spring adorned the beauty-burdened spray;
Wind and rain and fervent heat, caressing,
   Lavished glory on that second May!

High it rose – no wingèd grief could sweep it;
   Sin was scared to distance with its shine;
Love, and its own life, had power to keep it
   From all wrong – from every blight but thine!

Cruel Death! The young leaves droop and languish;
   Evening's gentle air may still restore –
No! the morning sunshine mocks my anguish –
   Time, for me, must never blossom more!

Strike it down, that other boughs may flourish
   Where that perished sapling used to be;
Thus, at least, its mouldering corpse will nourish
   That from which it sprung – Eternity.

'O God of Heaven! The dream of horror'

O God of Heaven! The dream of horror,
The frightful dream is over now;
The sickened heart, the blasting sorrow,
The ghastly night, the ghastlier morrow,
   The aching sense of utter woe;

The burning tears that would keep welling,
   The groan that mocked at every tear
That burst from out their dreary dwelling,
As if each gasp were life expelling,
   But life was nourished by despair;

The tossing and the anguished pining;
   The grinding teeth and starting eye;
The agony of still repining,
When not a spark of hope was shining
   From gloomy fate's relentless sky;

The impatient rage, the useless shrinking
   From thoughts that yet could not be borne;
The soul that was for ever thinking,
Till nature, maddened, tortured, sinking,
   At last refused to mourn.

It's over now; and I am free,
And the ocean-wind is caressing me –
The wild wind from that wavy main
I never thought to see again.

Bless thee, bright sea and glorious dome,
And my own world, my spirit's home;
Bless thee, bless all – I cannot speak:
   My voice is choked, but not with grief;
And salt-drops from my haggard cheek
   Descend, like rain upon the heath.

How long they've wet a dungeon floor,
   Falling on flag-stones, damp and grey!
I used to weep, even in my sleep:
   The night was dreadful, like the day.

I used to weep when winter's snow
   Whirled through the grating stormily;
But then it was a calmer woe,
   For everything was drear to me.

The bitterest time, the worst of all,
  Was that in which the summer sheen
Cast a green lustre on the wall
  That told of fields of lovelier green.

Often I've sat down on the ground,
  Gazing up to that flush scarce seen,
Till, heedless of the darkness round,
  My soul has sought a land serene.

It sought the arch of heaven divine,
  The pure blue heaven with clouds of gold;
It sought thy father's home and mine
  As I remembered it of old.

Oh, even now too horribly
  Come back the feelings that would swell,
When with my face hid on my knee
  I strove the bursting groans to quell.

I flung myself upon the stone;
  I howled, and tore my tangled hair;
And then, when the first gust had flown,
  Lay in unspeakable despair.

Sometimes a curse, sometimes a prayer,
  Would quiver on my parched tongue;
But both without a murmur there
  Died in the breast from whence they sprung.

And so the day would fade on high,
  And darkness quench that lonely beam,
And slumber mould my misery
  Into some strange and spectral dream,
Whose phantom horrors made me know
The worst extent of human woe.

But this is past, and why return
O'er such a path to brood and mourn?
Shake off the fetters, break the chain,
And live and love and smile again.

The waste of youth, the waste of years,
   Departed in that dungeon thrall;
The gnawing grief, the hopeless tears:
   Forget them, oh, forget them all!

'How still, how happy! These are words'

How still, how happy! These are words
   That once would scarce agree together;
I loved the plashing of the surge,
   The changing heaven, the breezy weather,

More than smooth seas and cloudless skies,
   And solemn, soothing, softened airs,
That in the forest woke no sighs,
   And from the green spray shook no tears.

How still, how happy! Now I feel
   Where silence dwells is sweeter far
Than laughing mirth's most joyous swell,
   However pure its raptures are.

Come, sit down on this sunny stone;
   'Tis wintry light o'er flowerless moors –
But sit – for we are all alone,
   And clear expand heaven's breathless shores.

I could think, in the withered grass
   Spring's budding wreaths we might discern;
The violet's eye might shyly flash,
   And young leaves shoot among the fern.

It is but thought – full many a night
  The snow shall clothe those hills afar,
And storms shall add a drearier blight,
  And winds shall wage a wilder war,

Before the lark may herald in
  Fresh foliage, twined with blossoms fair,
And summer days again begin
  Their glory-haloed crown to wear.

Yet my heart loves December's smile
  As much as July's golden beam:
Then let me sit and watch the while
  The blue ice curdling on the stream.

'The starry night shall tidings bring'

The starry night shall tidings bring:
  Go out upon the breezy moor –
Watch for a bird with sable wing,
  And beak and talons dropping gore.

Look not around, look not beneath,
  But mutely trace its airy way –
Mark where it lights upon the heath;
  Then, wanderer, kneel thee down and pray.

What fortune may await thee there,
  I will not, and I dare not tell;
But Heaven is moved by fervent prayer,
  And God is mercy; fare thee well!

'How long will you remain? The midnight hour'

'How long will you remain? The midnight hour
Has tolled its last stroke from the minster tower.
Come, come: the fire is dead, the lamp burns low;
Your eyelids droop, a weight is on your brow;
Your cold hands hardly hold the weary pen;
Come: morn will give recovered strength again.'

'No: let me linger; leave me, let me be
A little longer in this reverie;
I'm happy now; and would you tear away
My blissful thought that never comes with day:
A vision dear, though false, for well my mind
Knows what a bitter waking waits behind?'

'Can there be pleasure in this shadowy room,
With windows yawning on intenser gloom,
And such a dreary wind so bleakly sweeping
Round walls where only you are vigil keeping?
Besides, your face has not a sign of joy;
And more than tearful sorrow fills your eye.

Look on those woods, look on that mountain lorn,
And think how changed they'll be to-morrow morn:
The doors of heaven expanding bright and blue;
The leaves, the green grass, sprinkled with the dew;
And white mists rising on the river's breast,
And wild birds bursting from their songless nest,
And your own children's merry voices chasing
The phantom ghost that pleasure has been raising.'

'Ay, speak of these; but can you tell me why
Day breathes such beauty over earth and sky,
And waking sounds revive, restore again
The hearts that all night long have throbbed with pain?
Is it not that the sunshine and the wind

Lure from itself the mourner's woe-worn mind,
And all the joyous music breathing by,
And all the splendours of that cloudless sky,
Re-give him shadowy gleams of infancy,
And draw his tired gaze from futurity?'

'All day I've toiled, but not with pain'

All day I've toiled, but not with pain,
In learning's golden mine;
And now at eventide again
The moonbeams softly shine.

There is no snow upon the ground,
No frost on wind or wave;
The south wind blew with gentlest sound
And broke their icy grave.

'Tis sweet to wander here at night
To watch the winter die,
With heart as summer sunshine light
And warm as summer sky.

O may I never lose the peace
That lulls me gently now,
Though time should change my youthful face,
And years should shade my brow!

True to myself, and true to all,
May I be healthful still,
And turn away from passion's call,
And curb my own wild will.

'I am the only being whose doom'

I am the only being whose doom
No tongue would ask, no eye would mourn;
I never caused a thought of gloom,
A smile of joy, since I was born.

In secret pleasure, secret tears,
This changeful life has slipped away,
As friendless after eighteen years,
As lone as on my natal day.

There have been times I cannot hide,
There have been times when this was drear,
When my sad soul forgot its pride
And longed for one to love me here.

But those were in the early glow
Of feelings since subdued by care;
And they have died so long ago,
I hardly now believe they were.

First melted off the hope of youth,
Then fancy's rainbow fast withdrew;
And then experience told me truth
In mortal bosoms never grew.

'Twas grief enough to think mankind
All hollow, servile, insincere;
But worse to trust to my own mind
And find the same corruption there.

'Shall Earth no more inspire thee'

Shall Earth no more inspire thee,
Thou lonely dreamer now?
Since passion may not fire thee
Shall Nature cease to bow?

Thy mind is ever moving
In regions dark to thee;
Recall its useless roving –
Come back and dwell with me.

I know my mountain breezes
Enchant and soothe thee still –
I know my sunshine pleases
Despite thy wayward will.

When day with evening blending
Sinks from the summer sky,
I've seen thy spirit bending
In fond idolatry.

I've watched thee every hour;
I know my mighty sway,
I know my magic power
To drive thy griefs away.

Few hearts to mortals given
On earth so wildly pine;
Yet none would ask a Heaven
More like this Earth than thine.

Then let my winds caress thee;
Thy comrade let me be –
Since nought beside can bless thee,
Return and dwell with me.

The Prisoner

A Fragment

In the dungeon-crypts, idly did I stray,
Reckless of the lives wasting there away;
'Draw the ponderous bars! open, Warder stern!'
He dared not say me nay – the hinges harshly turn.

'Our guests are darkly lodged,' I whisper'd, gazing through
The vault, whose grated eye showed heaven more grey than blue
(This was when glad spring laughed in awaking pride);
'Aye, darkly lodged enough!' returned my sullen guide.

Then, God forgive my youth; forgive my careless tongue;
I scoffed, as the chill chains on the damp flag-stones rung:
'Confined in triple walls, art thou so much to fear,
That we must bind thee down and clench thy fetters here?'

The captive raised her face, it was as soft and mild
As sculptured marble saint, or slumbering unwean'd child;
It was so soft and mild, it was so sweet and fair,
Pain could not trace a line, nor grief a shadow there!

The captive raised her hand and pressed it to her brow;
'I have been struck,' she said, 'and I am suffering now;
Yet these are little worth, your bolts and irons strong,
And, were they forged in steel, they could not hold me long.'

Hoarse laughed the jailor grim: 'Shall I be won to hear;
Dost think, fond, dreaming wretch, that *I* shall grant thy prayer?
Or, better still, wilt melt my master's heart with groans?
Ah! sooner might the sun thaw down these granite stones.

'My master's voice is low, his aspect bland and kind,
But hard as hardest flint, the soul that lurks behind;
And I am rough and rude, yet not more rough to see
Than is the hidden ghost that has its home in me.'

About her lips there played a smile of almost scorn,
'My friend,' she gently said, 'you have not heard me mourn;
When you my kindred's lives, *my* lost life, can restore,
Then may I weep and sue – but never, friend, before!

Still, let my tyrants know, I am not doomed to wear
Year after year in gloom, and desolate despair;
A messenger of Hope comes every night to me,
And offers for short life, eternal liberty.

He comes with western winds, with evening's wandering airs,
With that clear dusk of heaven that brings the thickest stars.
Winds take a pensive tone, and stars a tender fire,
And visions rise, and change, that kill me with desire.

Desire for nothing known in my maturer years,
When Joy grew mad with awe, at counting future tears.
When, if my spirit's sky was full of flashes warm,
I knew not whence they came, from sun, or thunder storm.

But, first, a hush of peace – a soundless calm descends;
The struggle of distress, and fierce impatience ends.
Mute music soothes my breast, unuttered harmony,
That I could never dream, till Earth was lost to me.

Then dawns the Invisible; the Unseen its truth reveals;
My outward sense is gone, my inward essence feels:
Its wings are almost free – its home, its harbour found,
Measuring the gulph, it stoops, and dares the final bound.

Oh, dreadful is the check – intense the agony –
When the ear begins to hear, and the eye begins to see;
When the pulse begins to throb, the brain to think again,
The soul to feel the flesh, and the flesh to feel the chain.

Yet I would lose no sting, would wish no torture less,
The more that anguish racks, the earlier it will bless;
And robed in fires of hell, or bright with heavenly shine,
If it but herald death, the vision is divine!'

She ceased to speak, and we, unanswering, turned to go –
We had no further power to work the captive woe:
Her cheek, her gleaming eye, declared that man had given
A sentence, unapproved, and overruled by Heaven.

'Fall, leaves, fall; die, flowers, away'

Fall, leaves, fall; die, flowers, away;
Lengthen night and shorten day;
Every leaf speaks bliss to me
Fluttering from the autumn tree.
I shall smile when wreaths of snow
Blossom where the rose should grow;
I shall sing when night's decay
Ushers in a drearier day.

'Riches I hold in light esteem'

Riches I hold in light esteem
And Love I laugh to scorn
And lust of Fame was but a dream
That vanished with the morn –

And if I pray, the only prayer
That moves my lips for me
Is – 'Leave the heart that now I bear
And give me liberty.'

Yes, as my swift days near their goal
'Tis all that I implore –
Through life and death a chainless soul
With courage to endure!

'No coward soul is mine'

No coward soul is mine,
No trembler in the world's storm-troubled sphere.
I see Heaven's glories shine
And Faith stands equal arming me from Fear.

O God within my breast,
Almighty ever-present Deity,
Life, that in me hast rest
As I, Undying Life, have power in Thee.

Vain are the thousand creeds
That move men's hearts, unutterably vain,
Worthless as withered weeds
Or idlest froth amid the boundless main.

To waken doubt in one
Holding so fast by thy infinity,
So surely anchored on
The steadfast rock of Immortality.

With wide-embracing love
Thy spirit animates eternal years,
Pervades and broods above,
Changes, sustains, dissolves, creates and rears.

Though Earth and moon were gone
And suns and universes ceased to be
And thou wert left alone
Every Existence would exist in thee.

There is not room for Death
Nor atom that his might could render void
Since thou art Being and Breath
And what thou art may never be destroyed.

'In the earth, the earth, thou shalt be laid'

In the earth, the earth, thou shalt be laid,
A grey stone standing over thee;
Black mould beneath thee spread
And black mould to cover thee.

'Well, there is rest there,
So fast come thy prophecy;
The time when my sunny hair
Shall with grass roots twinèd be.'

But cold, cold is that resting place,
Shut out from Joy and Liberty,
And all who loved thy living face
Will shrink from its gloom and thee.

'Not so: *here* the world is chill,
And sworn friends fall from me;
But *there*, they'll own me still
And prize my memory.'

Farewell, then, all that love,
All that deep sympathy:
Sleep on; heaven laughs above,
Earth never misses thee.

Turf-sod and tombstone drear
Part human company;
One heart broke only there –
That heart was worthy thee!

'O thy bright eyes must answer now'

O thy bright eyes must answer now,
When Reason, with a scornful brow,
Is mocking at my overthrow;
O thy sweet tongue must plead for me
And tell why I have chosen thee!

Stern Reason is to judgement come
Arrayed in all her forms of gloom:
Wilt thou my advocate be dumb?
No, radiant angel, speak and say
Why I did cast the world away;

Why I have persevered to shun
The common paths that others run;
And on a strange road journeyed on
Heedless alike of Wealth and Power –
Of Glory's wreath and Pleasure's flower.

These once indeed seemed Beings divine,
And they perchance heard vows of mine
And saw my offerings on their shrine –
But, careless gifts are seldom prized,
And mine were worthily despised;

So with a ready heart I swore
To seek their altar-stone no more,
And gave my spirit to adore
Thee, ever present, phantom thing –
My slave, my comrade, and my King!

A slave because I rule thee still;
Incline thee to my changeful will
And make thy influence good or ill –
A comrade, for by day and night
Thou art my intimate delight –

My Darling Pain that wounds and sears
And wrings a blessing out from tears
By deadening me to real cares;
And yet, a king – though prudence well
Have taught thy subject to rebel.

And am I wrong to worship where
Faith cannot doubt nor Hope despair
Since my own soul can grant my prayer?
Speak, God of Visions, plead for me
And tell why I have chosen thee!

'How beautiful the Earth is still'

How beautiful the Earth is still
To thee – how full of Happiness;
How little fraught with real ill
Or shadowy phantoms of distress;

How Spring can bring thee glory yet
And Summer win thee to forget
December's sullen time!
Why dost thou hold the treasure fast
Of youth's delight, when youth is past
And thou art near thy prime?

When those who were thy own compeers,
Equal in fortunes and in years,
Have seen their morning melt in tears,
To dull unlovely day;
Blest, had they died unproved and young
Before their hearts were wildly wrung,
Poor slaves, subdued by passions strong,
A weak and helpless prey!

'Because, I hoped while they enjoyed,
And by fulfilment, hope destroyed –
As children hope, with trustful breast,
I waited Bliss and cherished Rest.

'A thoughtful Spirit taught me soon
That we must long till life be done;
That every phase of earthly joy
Will always fade and always cloy –

'This I foresaw, and would not chase
The fleeting treacheries,
But with firm foot and tranquil face
Held backward from the tempting race,
Gazed o'er the sands the waves efface
To the enduring seas –

'There cast my anchor of Desire
Deep in unknown Eternity;
Nor ever let my Spirit tire
With looking for *What is to be.*

'It is Hope's spell that glorifies
Like youth to my maturer eyes
All Nature's million mysteries –
The fearful and the fair –

'Hope soothes me in the griefs I know,
She lulls my pain for others' woe
And makes me strong to undergo
What I am born to bear.

'Glad comforter, will I not brave
Unawed the darkness of the grave?
Nay, smile to hear Death's billows rave,
My Guide, sustained by thee?
The more unjust seems present fate

The more my Spirit springs elate
Strong in thy strength, to anticipate
Rewarding Destiny!'

'Fair sinks the summer evening now'

Fair sinks the summer evening now
    In softened glory round my home;
The sky upon its holy brow
    Wears not a cloud that speaks of gloom.

The old tower, shrined in golden light,
    Looks down on the descending sun;
So gently evening blends with night,
    You scarce can say that day is done.

And this is just the joyous hour
    When we were wont to burst away,
To 'scape from labour's tyrant power
    And cheerfully go out to play.

Then why is all so sad and lone?
    No merry foot-step on the stair;
No laugh – no heart-awaking tone,
    But voiceless silence everywhere?

I've wandered round our garden-ground,
    And still it seemed at every turn
That I should greet approaching feet,
    And words upon the breezes borne.

In vain – they will not come to-day;
    And morning's beam will rise as drear:
Then tell me – are they gone for aye?
    Our sun blinks through the mists of care.

'Ah no,' reproving hope doth say,
'Departed joys 'tis fond to mourn,
When every storm that rides this way
Prepares a more divine return.'

JULIA WARD HOWE
1819–1910

Julia Ward Howe was the daughter of a wealthy New York banker,
Samuel Ward, and of an artistic and literary mother. Living in a grand
house with its own picture gallery in New York, she had a wonderful
education and a grand entry into New York society, but chose to marry
a man nearly twenty years her senior, a man of moral earnestness and
a strong social conscience, Samuel Grinley Howe. Her marriage
brought her into the world of Boston philosophers, poets, moralists
and Unitarians, and she met practically all the social reformers of
Massachusetts at that period.

She gave birth to five children in the first twelve years of marriage,
but found time to write copiously. With her husband, she became a
keen participant in the Abolitionist movement and helped him edit
The Commonwealth, an anti-slavery paper. Their Boston home
became a centre of the anti-slavery movement. During the Civil War
she visited an army camp with the party of Governor John Andrew of
Massachusetts, and was too tired and excited to sleep; instead she wrote
'Battle Hymn of the Republic', a remarkably stirring hymn which won
her instant and lasting fame and honour, but only four dollars in hard
cash!

Most of her poetry is hard reading these days, but her moral essays
are saved from utterly dull worthiness by a sense of humour which
keeps popping up at unlikely moments. Julia Ward Howe was a woman
of great spirit and talent, and the 'Hymn' shows her talent for capturing
the public imagination.

Battle Hymn of the Republic

Mine eyes have seen the glory of the coming of the Lord,
He is trampling out the vintage where the grapes of wrath are stored;
He hath loosed the fateful lightning of his terrible swift sword,
    His truth is marching on.

I have seen him in the watch-fires of a hundred circling camps,
They have builded him an altar in the evening dews and damps;
I can read his righteous sentence by the dim and flaring lamps,
    His day is marching on.

I have read a fiery gospel writ in burnished rows of steel:
'As ye deal with my contemners, so with you my grace shall deal;
Let the hero, born of woman, crush the serpent with his heel,
    Since God is marching on.'

He has sounded forth the trumpet that shall never call retreat,
He is sifting out the hearts of men before his judgment seat.
Oh, be swift, my soul, to answer him! be jubilant, my feet!
    Our God is marching on.

In the beauty of the lilies, Christ was born across the sea,
With a glory in his bosom that transfigures you and me;
As he died to make men holy, let us die to set men free,
    While God is marching on.

ANNE BRONTË
1820–1849

Anne was the youngest of the Brontë children. She was born just before
her father was appointed curate of Haworth, and the family moved
there shortly afterwards, where her gentle and sickly mother, Maria,
took to her bed and died.

Anne is the least well-known of the family, overshadowed by her sisters and her colourful brother Branwell. In a preface she wrote to Anne's first novel, *Agnes Grey*, Charlotte wrote of her youngest sister: 'Anne's character was milder and more subdued [than Emily's]; she wanted the power, the fire, the originality of her sister, but was well-endowed with great virtues of her own. Long-suffering, self-denying, reflective and intelligent, a constitutional reserve placed and kept her in the shade, and covered her mind and especially her feelings with a sort of nun-like veil which was never lifted . . .'

Some of Anne's poetry contains a depressing Calvinism. She became increasingly convinced that she was not part of the 'elect', and agonised over that. But she was torn between the strong Calvinist tradition and the sense that God could not be so cruel, so unloving, as to allow the arbitrary damning of creatures he himself had created. And so she wrote the most moving of all her poems, 'A Word to the "Elect"', in which she rails against the system by which the elect are elect through no virtue of their own, and suggests they think about the unfairness in that situation. Anne is a less elegant poet than her sisters, but there is still much that is worth reading in her poems, and her irritation with Calvinism and equal sense of assurance of divine protection make for fascinating study.

A Word to the 'Elect'*

You may rejoice to think *yourselves* secure;
You may be grateful for the gift divine –
That grace unsought, which made your black hearts pure,
And fits your earth-born souls in Heaven to shine.

But, is it sweet to look around, and view
Thousands excluded from that happiness
Which they deserve at least as much as you,–
Their faults not greater, nor their virtues less?

* The title in the original manuscript is 'A Word to the Calvinists'

And, wherefore should you love your God the more,
Because to you alone His smiles are given;
Because He chose to pass the *many* o'er,
And only bring the favoured *few* to Heaven?

And, wherefore should your hearts more grateful prove,
Because for *all* the Saviour did not die?
Is yours the God of justice and of love?
And are your bosoms warm with charity?

Say, does your heart expand to all mankind?
And, would you ever to your neighbour do –
The weak, the strong, the enlightened, and the blind –
As you would have your neighbour do to you?

And, when you, looking on your fellow-men,
Behold them doomed to endless misery,
How can you talk of joy and rapture then? –
May God withhold such cruel joy from me!

That none deserve eternal bliss I know;
Unmerited the grace in mercy given:
But none shall sink to everlasting woe,
That have not well deserved the wrath of Heaven.

And, oh! there lives within my heart
    A hope, long nursed by me;
(And should its cheering ray depart,
    How dark my soul would be!)

That as in Adam all have died,
    In Christ shall all men live;
And ever round His throne abide,
    Eternal praise to give.

That even the wicked shall at last
  Be fitted for the skies;
And when their dreadful doom is past,
  To life and light arise.

I ask not how remote the day,
  Nor what the sinners' woe,
Before their dross is purged away;
  Enough for me, to know

That when the cup of wrath is drained,
  The metal purified,
They'll cling to what they once disdained,
  And live by Him that died.

The Doubter's Prayer

Eternal Power, of earth and air!
Unseen, yet seen in all around,
Remote, but dwelling everywhere,
Though silent, heard in every sound.

If e'er Thine ear in mercy bent,
When wretched mortals cried to Thee,
And if, indeed, Thy Son was sent,
To save lost sinners such as me:

Then hear me now, while, kneeling here,
I lift to Thee my heart and eye,
And all my soul ascends in prayer,
Oh, give me - give me Faith! I cry.

Without some glimmering in my heart,
I could not raise this fervent prayer;
But, oh! a stronger light impart,
And in Thy mercy fix it there.

While Faith is with me, I am blest;
It turns my darkest night to day;
But while I clasp it to my breast,
I often feel it slide away.

Then, cold and dark, my spirit sinks,
To see my light of life depart;
And every fiend of Hell, methinks,
Enjoys the anguish of my heart.

What shall I do, if all my love,
My hopes, my toil, are cast away,
And if there be no God above,
To hear and bless me when I pray?

If this be vain delusion all,
If death be an eternal sleep,
And none can hear my secret call,
Or see the silent tears I weep!

Oh, help me, God! For Thou alone
Canst my distracted soul relieve;
Forsake it not: it is Thine own,
Though weak, yet longing to believe.

Oh, drive these cruel doubts away;
And make me know that Thou art God!
A faith, that shines by night and day,
Will lighten every earthly load.

If I believe that Jesus died,
And, waking, rose to reign above;
Then surely Sorrow, Sin, and Pride,
Must yield to Peace, and Hope, and Love.

And all the blessèd words He said
Will strength and holy joy impart:
A shield of safety o'er my head,
A spring of comfort in my heart.

A Prayer

My God (oh, let me call Thee mine,
    Weak, wretched sinner though I be),
My trembling soul would fain be Thine;
    My feeble faith still clings to Thee.

Not only for the past I grieve,
    The future fills me with dismay;
Unless Thou hasten to relieve,
    Thy suppliant is a castaway.

I cannot say my faith is strong,
    I dare not hope my love is great;
But strength and love to Thee belong:
    Oh, do not leave me desolate!

I know I owe my all to Thee;
    Oh, take the heart I cannot give;
Do Thou my Strength, my Saviour be,
    And make me to Thy glory live!

If This Be All

O God! if this indeed be all
    That Life can show to me;
If on my aching brow may fall
    No freshening dew from Thee,

If with no brighter light than this
   The lamp of hope may glow,
And I may only *dream* of bliss,
   And wake to weary woe;

If friendship's solace must decay,
   When other joys are gone,
And love must keep so far away,
   While I go wandering on, –

Wandering and toiling without gain,
   The slave of others' will,
With constant care and frequent pain,
   Despised, forgotten still;

Grieving to look on vice and sin,
   Yet powerless to quell
The silent current from within,
   The outward torrent's swell;

While all the good I would impart,
   The feelings I would share,
Are driven backward to my heart,
   And turned to wormwood there;

If clouds must *ever* keep from sight
   The glories of the Sun,
And I must suffer Winter's blight,
   Ere Summer is begun:

If Life must be so full of care,
   Then call me soon to Thee;
Or give me strength enough to bear
   My load of misery.

Vanitas Vanitatum, Omnia Vanitas

In all we do, and hear, and see,
Is restless Toil and Vanity.
While yet the rolling earth abides,
Men come and go like ocean tides;

And ere one generation dies,
Another in its place shall rise;
That, sinking soon into the grave,
Others succeed, like wave on wave;

And as they rise, they pass away.
The sun arises every day,
And, hastening onward to the West,
He nightly sinks, but not to rest:

Returning to the eastern skies,
Again to light us, he must rise.
And still the restless wind comes forth,
Now blowing keenly from the North;

Now from the South, the East, the West,
For ever changing, ne'er at rest.
The fountains, gushing from the hills,
Supply the ever-running rills;

The thirsty rivers drink their store,
And bear it rolling to the shore,
But still the ocean craves for more.
'Tis endless labour everywhere!
Sound cannot satisfy the ear,

Light cannot fill the craving eye,
Nor riches half our wants supply;
Pleasure but doubles future pain,
And joy brings sorrow in her train;

Laughter is mad, and reckless mirth –
What does she in this weary earth?
Should Wealth, or Fame, our Life employ,
Death comes, our labour to destroy;

To snatch the untasted cup away,
For which we toiled so many a day.
What, then, remains for wretched man?
To use life's comforts while he can,

Enjoy the blessings Heaven bestows,
Assist his friends, forgive his foes;
Trust God, and keep His statutes still,
Upright and firm, through good and ill;

Thankful for all that God has given,
Fixing his firmest hopes on Heaven;
Knowing that earthly joys decay,
But hoping through the darkest day.

Farewell to Thee! But Not Farewell

Farewell to thee! but not farewell
 To all my fondest thoughts of thee:
Within my heart they still shall dwell;
 And they shall cheer and comfort me.

O beautiful, and full of grace!
 If thou hadst never met mine eye,
I had not dreamed a living face
 Could fancied charms so far outvie.

If I may ne'er behold again
 That form and face so dear to me,
Nor hear thy voice, still would I fain
 Preserve for aye their memory.

That voice, the magic of whose tone
  Could wake an echo in my breast,
Creating feelings that, alone,
  Can make my trancèd spirit blest.

That laughing eye, whose sunny beam
  My memory would not cherish less;
And oh, that smile! whose joyous gleam
  No mortal language can express.

Adieu! but let me cherish still
  The hope with which I cannot part.
Contempt may wound, and coldness chill,
  But still it lingers in my heart.

And who can tell but Heaven, at last,
  May answer all my thousand prayers,
And bid the future pay the past
  With joy for anguish, smiles for tears.

Despondency

I have gone backward in the work,
  The labour has not sped;
Drowsy and dark my spirit lies,
  Heavy and dull as lead.

How can I rouse my sinking soul
  From such a lethargy?
How can I break these iron chains
  And set my spirit free?

There have been times when I have mourned
  In anguish o'er the past,
And raised my suppliant hands on high,
  While tears fell thick and fast;

And prayed to have my sins forgiven,
  With such a fervent zeal,
An earnest grief – a strong desire,
  That now I cannot feel.

And vowed to trample on my sins,
  And called on Heaven to aid
My spirit in her firm resolves
  And hear the vows I made.

And I have felt so full of love,
  So strong in spirit then,
As if my heart would never cool,
  Or wander back again.

And yet, alas! how many times
  My feet have gone astray,
How oft have I forgot my God,
  How greatly fallen away!

My sins increase, my love grows cold,
  And Hope within me dies;
And Faith itself is wavering now;
  Oh, how shall I arise?

I cannot weep, but I can pray,
  Then let me not despair;
Lord Jesus, save me, lest I die;
  Christ, hear my humble prayer!

To Cowper

Sweet are thy strains, celestial Bard;
  And oft, in childhood's years,
I've read them o'er and o'er again,
  With floods of silent tears.

The language of my inmost heart
　I traced in every line;
My sins, my sorrows, hopes, and fears,
　Were there – and only mine.

All for myself the sigh would swell,
　The tear of anguish start;
I little knew what wilder woe
　Had filled the Poet's heart.

I did not know the nights of gloom,
　The days of misery;
The long, long years of dark despair,
　That crushed and tortured thee.

But they are gone; from earth at length
　Thy gentle soul is passed,
And in the bosom of its God
　Has found its home at last.

It must be so, if God is love,
　And answers fervent prayer;
Then surely thou shalt dwell on high,
　And I may meet thee there.

Is He the source of every good,
　The spring of purity?
Then in thine hours of deepest woe,
　Thy God was still with thee.

How else, when every hope was fled,
　Couldst thou so fondly cling
To holy things and holy men?
　And how so sweetly sing

Of things that God alone could teach?
    And whence that purity,
That hatred of all sinful ways –
    That gentle charity?

Are *these* the symptoms of a heart
    Of heavenly grace bereft:
For ever banished from its God,
    To Satan's fury left?

Yet, should thy darkest fears be true,
    If Heaven be so severe,
That such a soul as thine is lost –
    Oh! how shall *I* appear?

Last Lines*

A dreadful darkness closes in
    On my bewildered mind;
O let me suffer and not sin,
    Be tortured yet resigned.

Through all this world of blinding mist
    Still let me look to Thee,
And give me courage to resist
    The Tempter till he flee.

Weary I am, O give me strength
    And leave me not to faint;
Say Thou wilt comfort me at length
    And pity my complaint.

---

* These are the last verses written by Anne Brontë, finished in January 1849, a few
months before her death.

I've begged to serve Thee heart and soul,
    To sacrifice to Thee
No niggard portion, but the whole
    Of my identity.

I hoped amid the brave and strong
    My portioned task might lie,
To toil amid the labouring throng
    With purpose keen and high.

But Thou hast fixed another part,
    And Thou hast fixed it well;
I said so with my breaking heart
    When first the anguish fell.

O Thou hast taken my delight
    And hope of life away,
And bid me watch the painful night
    And wait the weary day.

The hope and the delight were Thine:
    I bless Thee for their loan;
I gave Thee while I deemed them mine
    Too little thanks I own.

Shall I with joy Thy blessings share
    And not endure their loss,
Or hope the martyr's Crown to wear
    And cast away the Cross?

These weary hours will not be lost,
    These days of passive misery,
These nights of darkness, anguish-tost,
    If I can fix my heart on Thee.

The wretch that weak and weary lies
  Crushed with sorrow, worn with pain,
Still to Heaven may lift his eyes
  And strive and labour not in vain.

Weak and weary though I lie
  Crushed with sorrow, worn with pain,
I may lift to Heaven mine eye
  And strive and labour not in vain.

That inward strife against the sins
  That ever wait on suffering
To strike wherever first begins
  Each ill that would corruption bring;

That secret labour to sustain
  With humble patience every blow;
To gather fortitude from pain
  And hope and holiness from woe.

Thus let me serve Thee from my heart
  Whate'er may be my written fate,
Whether thus early to depart
  Or yet a while to wait.

If Thou shouldst bring me back to life,
  More humbled I should be,
More wise, more strengthened for the strife,
  More apt to lean on Thee.

Should death be standing at the gate,
  Thus should I keep my vow,
But hard whate'er my future fate,
  So let me serve Thee now.

AUGUSTA THEODOSIA DRANE
1823-1894

The youngest daughter of Thomas Drane, of the East India Mercantile Company, and his wife Cecilia, Augusta Theodosia Drane was born at Bromley St Leonard's, Middlesex, but the family moved to Babbicombe in Devon when she was fourteen. She was strongly influenced by the tractarian teaching at Torquay, and, after much thought and anxiety, she entered the Roman Catholic church at Tiverton in 1850. By this time she had published an essay often attributed to Newman, questioning the tractarian position.

In 1851, she went to Rome for six months and returned to be received as a postulant at the Dominican convent in Clifton, near Bristol. She was clothed in habit a few months later, and moved with all the other novices to Stone in Staffordshire in 1853. She pronounced her vows in 1856 and went on to become prioress of Stone from 1872 to 1881, and mother provincial of the order from 1872 to 1894. She died in her convent.

In the course of her life she wrote a great deal of theological material as well as a large number of poems, largely religious in nature. She is now almost unknown in Britain, yet her poetry is superb, and her prose writing fascinating. She is due for a revival.

Forgotten among the Lilies

> I fainted away abandoned;
> And amid the lilies forgotten
> Threw all my cares away.
> *St John of the Cross. The Obscure Night,* Stanza viii

Through the dark night I wander on alone,
And, as one blinded, grope my weary way,
Without a lamp to shed its guiding ray;
I wander on unseen, and seeing none,
And caring to behold but only One.

I see not, yet my heart will give me light,
And safer than the noonday sun will guide
To where the Bridegroom waiteth for the Bride;
So walking on in faith and not by sight,
I cannot fear but He will guide me right . . .

Forgotten 'mid the lilies; for I feel
Their gentle blossoms wave above my head;
I breathe the magic perfume which they shed,
As though my bleeding wounds they fain would heal,
And from my heart its aching sorrow steal.

A sad, sweet lot – I needs must call it sweet;
My cares, like withered buds, I cast aside,
And reck but little what may next betide;
The days and years fly past on pinions fleet,
Amid these lilies crushed beneath His feet.

Forgotten and abandoned; yet withal
Leaning my heart upon my only Love:
Nay, raise me not, I do not care to move;
Soon I shall hear His gentle footstep fall,
And lift my eyes, and answer to His call.

Till then among the lilies let me lie;
See, I have cast my idle cares away:
Howe'er it be, I am content to stay
Until once more the Bridegroom passes by,
And hither turns His gracious, pitying eye.

Blame not my folly, for I know for well
My words can nought but idle babbling seem,
The madness of a fond and foolish dream:
Bear with my folly, for the thoughts that swell
This burning heart, I cannot, dare not tell.

Know only this – I suffer, yet I rest;
For all my cares and fears are cast away,
And more than this I know not how to say;
Forgotten though I be, I own it best
And 'mid the lilies lie in perfect rest.

FRANCES W. HARPER
1825-1911

Frances Harper was born in Baltimore, Maryland, to free black parents.
Orphaned at an early age, she was brought up by an aunt and uncle who
were active in the anti-slavery movement and she herself became a
sought-after spokesperson for the cause. She was the author of the first
novel published by a black American woman, and the most popular
black poet of her day. She became self-supporting at the age of thirteen,
working as a seamstress, nursemaid and teacher before finding that her
true vocation was on the lecture platform. She made her first speech,
entitled 'The education and elevation of the colored race', in 1854, and
continued along similar themes. Her poetry is simple, direct and
appealing, and formed the highlight of her lectures.

Frances Harper continued to write all her life. Much of her poetry is
overly sentimental, sweetly religious and far from the modern taste.
But it is essential to read her poems aloud to get their rhythm. There
is in them almost a dance, certainly a song, and her best poems are
moving and simple, and occasionally very funny.

She's Free

How say that by law we may torture and chase
A woman whose crime is the hue of her face? –
With her step on the ice, and her arm on her child,

The danger was fearful, the pathway was wild . . .
But she's free! yes, free from the land where the slave,
From the hand of oppression, must rest in the grave;
Where bondage and blood, where scourges and chains,
Have placed on our banner indelible stains . . .
The bloodhounds have miss'd the scent of her way,
The hunter is rifled and foiled of his prey,
The cursing of men and clanking of chains
Make sounds of strange discord on Liberty's plains . . .
Oh! poverty, danger and death she can brave,
For the child of her love is no longer a slave.

Vashti

She leaned her head upon her hand
    And heard the King's decree –
'My lords are feasting in my halls;
    Bid Vashti come to me.

'I've shown the treasures of my house,
    My costly jewels rare,
But with the glory of her eyes
    No rubies can compare.

'Adorned and crowned, I'd have her come,
    With all her queenly grace
And mid my lords and mighty men
    Unveil her lovely face.

'Each gem that sparkles in my crown,
    Or glitters on my throne,
Grows poor and pale when she appears,
    My beautiful, my own!'

All waiting stood the chamberlains
  To hear the Queen's reply.
They saw her cheek grow deathly pale,
  But light flashed to her eye:

'Go, tell the King,' she proudly said,
  'That I am Persia's Queen,
And by his crowd of merry men
  I never will be seen.

'I'll take the crown from off my head,
  And tread it 'neath my feet,
Before their rude and careless gaze
  My shrinking eyes shall meet.

'A Queen unveiled before the crowd!
  Upon each lip my name! –
Why, Persia's women all would blush
  And weep for Vashti's shame.

'Go back!' she cried, and waved her hand,
  And grief was in her eye:
'Go tell the King,' she sadly said,
  'That I would rather die.'

They brought her message to the King;
  Dark flashed his angry eye;
'Twas as the lightning ere the storm
  Hath swept in fury by.

Then bitterly outspoke the King,
  Through purple lips of wrath –
'What shall be done to her who dares
  To cross your monarch's path?'

Then spake his wily counsellors –
'O, King of this fair land,
From distant Ind to Ethiop,
All bow to thy command.

'But if, before thy servants' eyes,
This thing they plainly see,
That Vashti doth not heed thy will
Nor yield herself to thee.

'The women, restive 'neath our rule,
Would learn to scorn our name,
And from her deed to us would come
Reproach and burning shame.

'Then, gracious King, sign with thy hand
This stern but just decree,
That Vashti lay aside her crown,
Thy Queen no more to be.'

She heard again the King's command,
And left her high estate;
Strong in her earnest womanhood,
She calmly met her fate,

And left the palace of the King,
Proud of her spotless name –
A woman who could bend to grief
But would not bend to shame.

EMILY PFEIFFER
1827–1890

Emily Pfeiffer had relatively little formal education because her father lost most of his money. She was therefore educated at home, and she was what the Victorians described as 'delicate' and subject to depression. Her first volume was *The Holly Branch: An Album for 1843*, an anthology of her own poems and stories, and she continued producing volume after volume of poetry after her marriage to Juergern Edward Pfeiffer in 1853. Much of her work betrays her keen interest in women's issues, as does her legacy to further women's higher education. But there is also a significant concern with her feelings about Christianity, and a growing devotional aspect to her poetry the older she becomes.

The Hunger of Life

If Life is but a hunger to attain –
  A longing for some unattested Good,
  Whose secret has been whispered to the blood
Which bears upon its way each gathered gain,
And leaves our questionings in dumb disdain,
  Then in fulfilment, life itself must cease,
  Nearer to death related than to peace,
And as it slowly waxed, must slowly wane.

Dim consciousness, whose cradle was the ocean,
  How high art thou uplifted since thy birth!
On the twin arches of man's feet, his motion
  Is as a god's upon the subject earth;
Life hath fulfilled itself, played out its part:
Will refluent hunger turn to eat its heart?

The Gospel of Dread Tidings

If that sad creed which honest men and true
　Are flouting in the cheerful face of Day,
　Are teaching in the schools, and by the way –
Tho' only guesses on a broken clue –
If such should in the end quench all the blue
　Above us, then the saddest souls were they
　Who knew and loved the most, and could not lay
The ghost of Hope, and hold the grave in lieu.

O Christ, Thou highest man! if it were so,
　And Thou couldst see it, that great heart of Thine
　　Would burn to come amongst us – not to preach
Thy law again, or set our loves a-glow,
　Still less in glory – but to blot each line,
Each thought, each word, Thou camest first to teach.

The Winged Soul

My soul is like some cage-born bird, that hath
　A restless prescience – howsoever won –
　Of a broad pathway leading to the sun,
With promptings of an oft-reprovèd faith
In sun-ward yearnings. Stricken though her breast,
　And faint her wing with beating at the bars
　Of sense, she looks beyond outlying stars,
And only in the Infinite sees rest.

Sad soul! If ever thy desire be bent
　Or broken to thy doom, and made to share
The ruminant's beatitude – content –
　Chewing the cud of knowledge, with no care
For germs of life within; *then* will I say,
Thou art not caged, but fitly *stalled* in clay!

The 'Sting of Death'

O thou whom men affirm we cannot know,
  It may be we may never see Thee nearer
  Than 'in the clouds', nor ever trace Thee clearer
Than in that garment which, howe'er aglow
With love divine, is still a changing show,
  A little shadowing forth, and more concealing,
  A glory which, in uttermost revealing,
Might strike us dead with one supreme life-blow.

We may not reach Thee through the void immense
  Measured by suns, or prove Thee anywhere,
  But hungry eyes that hunt the wilds above
For one lost face, still drop despairing thence
  To find Thee in the heart – life's ravished lair –
  Else were the 'sting of death' not sin, but love!

A Protest

Let no man charge thee, woman if thou art,
  And therefore pitiful, to veil thine eyes
  From any naked truth whereof the cries
Reveal the anguish. Woman to the heart –
There be foul shames which for thy purer part
  Appear through bleeding wounds in purple guise,
  And at their aspect, showing in such wise,
No whitest angel of God's throne would start.

And more; if it be true that life terrene,
Mocking our hope, admits a depth obscene,
  Wherein lost souls must fall to mend our ways;
Feed full that gulf of hell which is man's lust,
But rob not those its devotees; be just:
  Cheer its frail victims; give its martyrs praise!

Sweet Christ! That there be men in virtue's name
   And Thine, would levy on Thy 'poor' a toll
   Whereof each fraction is a living soul
To drop in stygian depths of sin and shame.
O, vainly lost ones! If of our fair fame,
   Our woman's peace and purity, the whole
   Fierce chastisement is laid on you, your dole
Brands our white brows with more than answering blame.

From such salvation, turning in despair,
   They well might sigh for cloistered days, who dare
   Not walk without such guardians of the night!
God help the braver hearted to allay
The torments of these damned, until they may
   Pluck from the rose of innocence this blight.

And you, the queens who claim to reign in right
   Of this foul wrong; you who from thought would spurn
   Your hapless hostages; how do *you* earn
The service you so hardly would requite?
Have you emerged like stars from some dark night
   Of ignorance, or compassed a return
   From sin foredoomed? What wonders may we learn
From you of deadly hunger's conquered might?

Alas! on simpler plea your titles rest:
   For these to float it needs that those must drown;
And you who ride upon the waves' high crest,
   Whose thoughts are narrowed by your unearned crown,
   How should it irk you if the partial frown
Of Him you worship, banned whom Jesus blest?

HELEN HUNT JACKSON
1830–1885

Along with Emily Dickinson, Helen Jackson was another native of Amherst, Massachusetts. Her father taught classics and moral philosophy at Amherst College, and her mother died young of TB in 1844. She and Emily Dickinson were neighbours and early schoolfellows and became lifelong friends. Helen married Edward Bissell Hunt in 1852, and they led the roving life of a military family on active service. In 1863 Edward was killed while experimenting with one of his own inventions, a submarine sea-projector entitled a 'sea-miner'. Their first child died at eleven months, and their second, Warren Horsford, known as 'Rennie', died in 1865. Her parents, husband and sons dead, Helen Jackson was left utterly bereft.

She moved to Newport, Rhode Island, where she met T. W. Higginson, who encouraged her writing. Her first poem was published in *The Nation* just after Warren's death, and she continued to write and be published throughout the 1860s and early '70s.

In 1873–4 she spent the winter at the Colorado Springs Hotels to cope with her bronchial trouble. There she met the banker, financier and railway manager, William Sharpless Jackson, whom she married in 1875. She remained in Colorado Springs for the rest of her life, writing increasingly about the wrongs done to American Indians. In 1882 she became a government commissioner, with a brief to investigate the needs and conditions of the Mission Indians of California. When she felt that no action had been taken as a result of her report, she turned to fiction and published *Ramona*, indicting the government's cruelty and treachery.

For the few remaining years of her life she was a keen writer of verse, plays and fiction, but such was her obsession with secrecy and privacy that many of her works remained unsigned. Her contributions to the cause of American Indians and to American literary life are known to be considerable, but the exact extent of the latter is unclear.

Habeas Corpus*

My body, eh? Friend Death, how now?
　Why all this tedious pomp of writ?
Thou hast reclaimed it sure and slow
　For half a century, bit by bit.

In faith thou knowest more to-day
　Than I do, where it can be found!
This shriveled lump of suffering clay,
　To which I now am chained and bound,

Has not of kith or kin a trace
　To the good body once I bore;
Look at this shrunken, ghastly face:
　Didst ever see that face before?

Ah, well, friend Death, good friend thou art;
　Thy only fault thy lagging gait,
Mistaken pity in thy heart
　For timorous ones that bid thee wait.

Do quickly all thou hast to do,
　Nor I nor mine will hindrance make;
I shall be free when thou art through;
　I grudge thee naught that thou must take!

Stay! I have lied: I grudge thee one,
　Yes, two I grudge thee at this last –
Two members which have faithful done
　My will and bidding in the past.

---

* Her last poem: 7 August 1885

I grudge thee this right hand of mine;
  I grudge thee this quick-beating heart;
They never gave me coward sign,
  Nor played me once a traitor's part.

I see now why in olden days
  Men in barbaric love or hate
Nailed enemies' hands at wild crossways,
  Shrined leaders' hearts in costly state:

The symbol, sign, and instrument
  Of each soul's purpose, passion, strife,
Of fires in which are poured and spent
  Their all of love, their all of life.

O feeble, mighty human hand!
  O fragile, dauntless human heart!
The universe holds nothing planned
  With such sublime, transcendent art!

Yes, Death, I own I grudge thee mine
  Poor little hand, so feeble now;
Its wrinkled palm, its altered line,
  Its veins so pallid and so slow –

[Unfinished here.]

Ah, well, friend Death, good friend thou art:
  I shall be free when thou art through.
Take all there is – take hand and heart:
  There must be somewhere work to do.

EMILY DICKINSON
1830–1886

Emily Dickinson was born into a distinguished family in Amherst, Massachusetts, a very proper, profoundly Christian New England small town. She was educated at Amherst Academy and at Mount Holyoke College (then entitled Female Seminary), the foremost women's college of her day, before returning to Amherst. She described her home town in a letter to Mrs Samuel Bowles: 'It storms in Amherst five days – it snows, and then it rains, and then soft fogs like vails hang on all the houses, and then the days turn Topaz, like a lady's pin . . .'

Apart from brief trips to visit friends, she never left her father's house again, and indeed spent much of her life in deliberate seclusion; although her brother's family lived next door, there was some estrangement and she did not often see them. Despite the fact that her family and friends knew about her poetry, she refused to allow much of it to be published during her lifetime.

It was after her death that her sister Lavinia found a box containing hundreds of poems, some carefully copied into booklets Emily had stitched herself, some scrawled on bits of paper, some on old shopping lists and the backs of envelopes. Although Lavinia destroyed many of the papers about Emily's life in the probably quite accurate belief that her sister would not have wanted the public to know anything about her, she restrained herself from destroying the poems, and they were listed and published in the following years.

There may have been a secret love in Emily's life, and there is much speculation in her biographies about her relationship with a local judge. Certainly some of her earlier poems concentrate on mortal and erotic love. But over the years this theme changes, becoming a mystical love of God, a fascination with death and a constant playing on the changing value set on life and death. She wrote large numbers of letters, of which relatively few survive. But among those which do are some to Thomas Wentworth Higginson, which bear witness to her love of the seventeenth-century mystical poets. One sentence records her belief that only the mind, and its creation, her poems, possesses 'a spectral power . . . that walks alone'.

She has retained her power to move, and her popularity has grown throughout this century, as the fascination with the unknown facets of her life grows too.

'I felt a Funeral, in my Brain'

I felt a Funeral, in my Brain,
And Mourners to and fro
Kept treading – treading – till it seemed
That Sense was breaking through –

And when they all were seated,
A Service, like a Drum –
Kept beating – beating – till I thought
My Mind was going numb –

And then I heard them lift a Box
And creak across my Soul
With those same Boots of Lead, again,
Then Space – began to toll,

As all the Heavens were a Bell,
And Being, but an Ear,
And I, and Silence, some strange Race
Wrecked, solitary, here –

And then a Plank in Reason, broke,
And I dropped down, and down –
And hit a World, at every plunge,
And Finished knowing – then –

'A Day! Help! Help! Another Day!'

A Day! Help! Help! Another Day!
Your prayers, oh Passer by!
From such a common ball as this
Might date a Victory!
From marshallings as simple
The flags of nations swang.
Steady – my soul: What issues
Upon thine arrow hang!

'There's something quieter than sleep'

There's something quieter than sleep
Within this inner room!
It wears a sprig upon its breast –
And will not tell its name.

Some touch it, and some kiss it –
Some chafe its idle hand –
It has a simple gravity
I do not understand!

I would not weep if I were they –
How rude in one to sob!
Might scare the quiet fairy
Back to her native wood!

While simple-hearted neighbors
Chat of the 'Early dead' –
We – prone to periphrasis,
Remark that Birds have fled!

'I never lost as much but twice'

I never lost as much but twice,
And that was in the sod.
Twice have I stood a beggar
Before the door of God!

Angels – twice descending
Reimbursed my store –
Burglar! Banker – Father!
I am poor once more!

Exclusion

The soul selects her own society,
    Then shuts the door;
On her divine majority
    Obtrude no more.

Unmoved, she notes the chariot's pausing
    At her low gate;
Unmoved, an emperor is kneeling
    Upon her mat.

I've known her from an ample nation
    Choose one;
Then close the valves of her attention
    Like stone.

'Going to Heaven!'

Going to Heaven!
I don't know when –
Pray do not ask me how!
Indeed I'm too astonished

To think of answering you!
Going to Heaven!
How dim it sounds!
And yet it will be done
As sure as flocks go home at night
Unto the Shepherd's arm!

Perhaps you're going too!
Who knows?
If you should get there first
Save just a little space for me
Close to the two I lost –
The smallest 'Robe' will fit me
And just a bit of 'Crown' –
For you know we do not mind our dress
When we are going home –

I'm glad I don't believe it
For it would stop my breath –
And I'd like to look a little more
At such a curious Earth!
I'm glad they did believe it
Whom I have never found
Since the mighty Autumn afternoon
I left them in the ground.

'Dust is the only Secret'

Dust is the only Secret –
Death, the only One
You cannot find out all about
In his 'native town'.

Nobody knew 'his Father' –
Never was a Boy –
Hadn't any playmates,
Or 'Early history' –

Industrious! Laconic!
Punctual! Sedate!
Bold as a Brigand!
Stiller than a Fleet!

Builds, like a Bird, too!
Christ robs the Nest –
Robin after Robin
Smuggled to Rest!

'Soul, wilt thou toss again?'

Soul, wilt thou toss again?
By just such a hazard
Hundreds have lost indeed –
But tens have won an all –

Angel's breathless ballot
Lingers to record thee –
Imps in eager Caucus
Raffle for my Soul!

'Tis so much joy! 'Tis so much joy!'

'Tis so much joy! 'Tis so much joy!
If I should fail, what poverty!
And yet, as poor as I,
Have ventured all upon a throw!
Have gained! Yes! Hesitated so –
This side the Victory!

Life is but Life! And Death, but Death!
Bliss is, but Bliss, and Breath but Breath!
And if indeed I fail,
At least, to know the worst, is sweet!
Defeat means nothing *but* Defeat,
No drearier, can befall!

And if I gain! Oh Gun at Sea!
Oh Bells, that in the Steeples be!
At first, repeat it slow!
For Heaven is a different thing,
Conjectured, and waked sudden in –
And might extinguish me!

'I lost a World – the other day!'

I lost a World – the other day!
Has Anybody found?
You'll know it by the Row of Stars
Around its forehead bound.

A Rich man – might not notice it –
Yet – to my frugal Eye,
Of more Esteem than Ducats –
Oh find it – Sir – for me!

'I live with Him – I see His face'

I live with Him – I see His face –
I go no more away
For Visitor – or Sundown –
Death's single privacy

The Only One - forestalling Mine -
And that - by Right that He
Presents a Claim invisible -
No wedlock - granted Me -

I live with Him - I hear His Voice -
I stand alive - Today -
To witness to the Certainty
Of Immortality -

Taught Me - by Time - the lower Way -
Conviction - Every day -
That Life like This - is stopless -
Be Judgment - what it may -

'I am ashamed - I hide'

I am ashamed - I hide -
What right have I - to be a Bride -
So late a Dowerless Girl -
Nowhere to hide my dazzled Face -
No one to teach me that new Grace -
Nor introduce - my Soul -

Me to adorn - How - tell -
Trinket - to make Me beautiful -
Fabrics of Cashmere -
Never a Gown of Dun - more -
Raiment instead - of Pompadour -
For Me - My soul - to wear -

Fingers – to frame my Round Hair
Oval – as Feudal Ladies wore –
Far Fashions – Fair –
Skill – to hold my Brow like an Earl –
Plead – like a Whippoorwill –
Prove – like a Pearl –
Then, for Character –

Fashion My Spirit quaint – white –
Quick – like a Liquor –
Gay – like Light –
Bring Me my best Pride –
No more ashamed –
No more to hide –
Meek – let it be – too proud – for Pride –
Baptized – this Day – A Bride –

'My period had come for Prayer'

My period had come for Prayer –
No other Art – would do –
My Tactics missed a rudiment –
Creator – Was it you?

God grows above – so those who pray
Horizons – must ascend –
And so I stepped upon the North
To see this Curious Friend –

His House was not – no sign had He –
By Chimney – nor by Door
Could I infer his Residence –
Vast Prairies of Air

Unbroken by a Settler –
Were all that I could see –
Infinitude – Had'st Thou no Face
That I might look on Thee?

The Silence condescended –
Creation stopped – for Me –
But awed beyond my errand –
I worshipped – did not 'pray' –

'Because I could not stop for Death'

Because I could not stop for Death –
He kindly stopped for me –
The Carriage held but just Ourselves –
And Immortality.

We slowly drove – He knew no haste
And I had put away
My labor and my leisure too,
For His Civility –

We passed the School, where Children strove
At Recess – in the Ring –
We passed the Fields of Gazing Grain –
We passed the Setting Sun –

Or rather – He passed Us –
The Dews drew quivering and chill –
For only Gossamer, my Gown –
My Tippet – only Tulle –

We paused before a House that seemed
A Swelling of the Ground –
The Roof was scarcely visible –
The Cornice – in the Ground –

Since then – 'tis Centuries – and yet
Feels shorter than the Day
I first surmised the Horses' Heads
Were toward Eternity –

'Wait till the Majesty of Death'

Wait till the Majesty of Death
Invests so mean a brow!
Almost a powdered Footman
Might dare to touch it now!

Wait till in Everlasting Robes
That Democrat is dressed,
Then prate about 'Preferment' –
And 'Station', and the rest!

Around this quiet Courtier
Obsequious Angels wait!
Full royal is his Retinue!
Full purple is his state!

A Lord, might dare to lift the Hat
To such a Modest Clay
Since that My Lord, 'the Lord of Lords'
Receives unblushingly!

'Behind Me – dips Eternity'

Behind Me – dips Eternity –
Before Me – Immortality –
Myself – the Term between –
Death but the Drift of Eastern Gray,
Dissolving into Dawn away,
Before the West begin –

'Tis Kingdoms – afterward – they say –
In perfect – pauseless Monarchy –
Whose Prince – is Son of None –
Himself – His Dateless Dynasty –
Himself – Himself diversify –
In Duplicate divine –

'Tis Miracle before Me – then –
'Tis Miracle behind – between –
A Crescent in the Sea –
With Midnight to the North of Her –
And Midnight to the South of Her –
And Maelstrom – in the Sky –

'It's easy to invent a Life'

It's easy to invent a Life –
God does it – every Day –
Creation – but the Gambol
Of His Authority –

It's easy to efface it –
The thifty Deity
Could scarce afford Eternity
To Spontaneity –

The Perished Patterns murmur –
But His Perturbless Plan
Proceed – inserting Here – a Sun –
There – leaving out a Man –

'My Worthiness is all my Doubt'

My Worthiness is all my Doubt –
His Merit – all my fear –
Contrasting which, my quality
Do lowlier – appear –

Lest I should insufficient prove
For His beloved Need –
The Chiefest Apprehension
Upon my thronging Mind –

'Tis true – that Deity to stoop
Inherently incline –
For nothing higher than Itself
Itself can rest upon –

So I – the undivine abode
Of His Elect Content –
Conform my Soul – as 'twere a Church,
Unto Her Sacrament –

'The going from a world we know'

The going from a world we know
    To one a wonder still
Is like the child's adversity
    Whose vista is a hill,

Behind the hill is sorcery
    And everything unknown,
But will the secret compensate
    For climbing it alone?

'Of God we ask one favor'

Of God we ask one favor,
That we may be forgiven –
For what, he is presumed to know –
The Crime, from us, is hidden –
Immured the whole of Life
Within a magic Prison
We reprimand the Happiness
That too competes with Heaven.

'Had I known that the first was the last'

Had I known that the first was the last
I should have kept it longer.
Had I known that the last was the first
I should have drunk it stronger.
Cup, it was your fault,
Lip was not the liar.
No, lip, it was yours,
Bliss was most to blame.

'He was my host – he was my guest'

He was my host – he was my guest,
I never to this day
If I invited him could tell,
Or he invited me.

So infinite our intercourse
So intimate, indeed,
Analysis as capsule seemed
To keeper of the seed.

'Dying! To be afraid of thee'

Dying! To be afraid of thee
One must to thine Artillery
Have left exposed a Friend –
Than thine old Arrow is a Shot
Delivered straighter to the Heart
The leaving Love behind.

Not for itself, the Dust is shy,
But, enemy, Beloved be
Thy Batteries divorce.
Fight sternly in a Dying eye
Two Armies, Love and Certainty
And Love and the Reverse.

'Death is like the insect'

Death is like the insect
Menacing the tree,
Competent to kill it,
But decoyed may be.

Bait it with the balsam,
Seek it with the saw,
Baffle, if it cost you
Everything you are.

Then, if it have burrowed
Out of reach of skill –
Wring the tree and leave it,
'Tis the vermin's will.

'A Pit – but Heaven over it'

A Pit – but Heaven over it –
And Heaven beside, and Heaven abroad,
And yet a Pit –
With Heaven over it.

To stir would be to slip –
To look would be to drop –
To dream – to sap the Prop
That holds my chances up.
Ah! Pit! With Heaven over it!

The depth is all my thought –
I dare not ask my feet –
'Twould start us where we sit
So straight you'd scarce suspect
It was a Pit – with fathoms under it –
Its Circuit just the same.
Seed – summer – tomb –
Whose Doom to whom?

'I took one Draught of Life'

I took one Draught of Life –
I'll tell you what I paid –
Precisely an existence –
The market price, they said.

They weighed me, Dust by Dust –
They balanced Film with Film,
Then handed me my Being's worth –
A single Dram of Heaven!

'The last night that she lived'

The last night that she lived,
It was a common night,
Except the dying; this to us
Made nature different.

We noticed smallest things, –
Things overlooked before,
By this great light upon our minds
Italicized, as 'twere.

That others could exist
While she must finish quite,
A jealousy for her arose
So nearly infinite.

We waited while she passed;
It was a narrow time,
Too jostled were our souls to speak,
At length the notice came.

She mentioned, and forgot;
Then lightly as a reed
Bent to the water, shivered scarce,
Consented, and was dead.

And we, we placed the hair,
And drew the head erect;
And then an awful leisure was,
Our faith to regulate.

CHRISTINA ROSSETTI
1830–1894

Christina Rossetti was the younger sister of the poet and Pre-Raphaelite painter Dante Gabriel Rossetti, and her early years were closely intertwined with his. They grew up in an impoverished, cultured, complicated household with much music and art around them. She wrote furiously, and published early fairy-tale poems in *The Germ*, a Pre-Raphaelite journal. She was very beautiful in a pale, serious way, and frequently acted as model for her brother's paintings, especially those of the Virgin. She adored the countryside and nature, as is clear from her poetry, but her religious beliefs became more and more priggish: in 1866 she refused a suitor because he was 'either not a Christian at all, or else he was a Christian of undefined or heterodox views'.

From 1861, after a trip to the continent, she was obliged to care for her parents and other invalid relatives; her life became more and more restricted and she was increasingly preoccupied with religious thoughts. Her own health deteriorated in 1871; she grew fat and was less and less able to go out. Eventually she became confined to her house in Bloomsbury, where she wrote in a back bedroom and conducted regular household devotions. She was extraordinarily brave throughout her illness, which proved to be cancer: although it became ever more painful in the years leading up to her death, she never alluded to it in conversation.

Her preoccupation with religion is apparent in her poetry, though she manages, in the space of rather confined, theological sonnets, to create some magic and a deep sense of spiritual awareness.

Remember

Remember me when I am gone away,
    Gone far away into the silent land;
    When you can no more hold me by the hand,
Nor I half turn to go yet turning stay.

Remember me when no more day by day
  You tell me of our future that you planned:
  Only remember me; you understand
It will be late to counsel then or pray.
Yet if you should forget me for a while
  And afterwards remember, do not grieve:
  For if the darkness and corruption leave
A vestige of the thoughts that once I had,
Better by far you should forget and smile
  Than that you should remember and be sad.

Mary Magdalene

She came in deep repentance,
  And knelt down at His feet
Who can change the sorrow into joy,
  The bitter into sweet.

She had cast away her jewels
  And her rich attire,
And her breast was filled with a holy shame,
  And her heart with a holy fire.

Her tears were more precious
  Than her precious pearls –
Her tears that fell upon His feet
  As she wiped them with her curls.

Her youth and her beauty
  Were budding to their prime;
But she wept for the great transgression,
  The sin of other time.

Trembling betwixt hope and fear,
  She sought the King of Heaven,
Forsook the evil of her ways,
  Loved much, and was forgiven.

The End of Time

  Thou who art dreary
With a cureless woe,
  Thou who art weary
Of all things below,
  Thou who art weeping
By the loved sick bed,
  Thou who art keeping
Watches o'er the dead –
Hope, hope! old Time flies fast upon his way,
And soon will cease the night, and soon will dawn the day.

  The rose blooms brightly,
But it fades ere night;
  And youth flies lightly,
Yet how sure its flight!
  And still the river
Merges in the sea;
  And Death reigns ever
Whilst old Time shall be –
Yet hope! old Time flies fast upon his way,
And soon will cease the night, and soon will dawn the day.

  All we most cherish
In this world below,
  What though it perish?
It has aye been so.
  So through all ages
It has ever been,
  To fools and sages,

Noble men and mean: –
Yet hope, still hope! for Time flies on his way,
And soon will end the night, and soon will dawn the day.

All of each nation
Shall that morning see
With exultation
Or with misery:
From watery slumbers,
From the opening sod,
Shall rise up numbers
To be judged by God.
Then hope and fear, for Time speeds on his way,
And soon must end the night, and soon must dawn the day.

Sweet Death

The sweetest blossoms die.
And so it was that, going day by day
Unto the Church to praise and pray,
And crossing the green churchyard thoughtfully,
I saw how on the graves the flowers
Shed their fresh leaves in showers,
And how their perfume rose up to the sky
Before it passed away.

The youngest blossoms die.
They die and fall and nourish the rich earth
From which they lately had their birth;
Sweet life, but sweeter death that passeth by
And is as though it had not been: –
All colours turn to green;
The bright hues vanish, and the odours fly,
The grass hath lasting worth.

And youth and beauty die.
  So be it, O my God, Thou God of Truth:
  Better than beauty and than youth
Are Saints and Angels, a glad company;
  And Thou, O Lord, our Rest and Ease,
  Art better far than these.
Why should we shrink from our full harvest? why
  Prefer to glean with Ruth?

From Songs for Strangers and Pilgrims

'What is that to thee? follow thou Me'

Lie still, my restive heart, lie still:
God's Word to thee saith, 'Wait and bear.'
The good which He appoints is good,
The good which He denies were ill:
Yea, subtle comfort is thy care,
Thy hurt a help not understood.

'Friend, go up higher,' to one: to one,
'Friend, enter thou My joy,' He saith:
To one, 'Be faithful unto death.'
For some a wilderness doth flower,
Or day's work in one hour is done: –
'But thou, couldst thou not watch one hour?'

Lord, I had chosen another lot,
But then I had not chosen well;
Thy choice and only Thine is good:
No different lot, search heaven or hell,
Had blessed me, fully understood;
None other, which Thou orderest not.

'Afterward he repented, and went'

Lord, when my heart was whole I kept it back
  And grudged to give it Thee.
Now then that it is broken, must I lack
  Thy kind word 'Give it Me'?
Silence would be but just, and Thou art just.
Yet since I lie here shattered in the dust,
  With still an eye to lift to Thee,
A broken heart to give,
I think that Thou wilt bid me live,
  And answer 'Give it Me.'

'A heavy heart, if ever heart was heavy'

A heavy heart, if ever heart was heavy,
  I offer Thee this heavy heart of me.
Are such as this the hearts Thou art fain to levy
  To do and dare for Thee, to bleed for Thee?
  Ah blessed heaviness if such they be!

Time was I bloomed with blossom and stood leafy,
  How long before the fruit if fruit there be:
Lord, if by bearing fruit my heart grows heavy,
  Leafless and bloomless yet accept of me
  The stripped fruit-bearing heart I offer Thee.

Lifted to Thee my heart weighs not so heavy,
  It leaps and lightens lifted up to Thee;
It sings, it hopes to sing amid the bevy
  Of thousand thousand choirs that sing, and see
  Thy Face, me loving, for Thou lovest me.

'Lord, grant us calm, if calm can set forth Thee'

Lord, grant us calm, if calm can set forth Thee;
  Or tempest, if a tempest set Thee forth;
  Wind from the east or west or south or north,

Or congelation of a silent sea,
With stillness of each tremulous aspen tree.
Still let fruit fall, or hang upon the tree;
    Still let the east and west, the south and north,
Curb in their winds, or plough a thundering sea;
    Still let the earth abide to set Thee forth,
Or vanish like a smoke to set forth Thee.

Behold, I Stand at the Door and Knock

Who standeth at the gate? – A woman old,
A widow from the husband of her love.
'O lady, stay, this wind is piercing cold,
    Oh look at the keen frosty moon above;
I have no home, am hungry, feeble, poor.' –
    'I'm really very sorry, but I can
    Do nothing for you; there's the clergyman,'
The lady said, and shivering closed the door

Who standeth at the gate? – Way-worn and pale
A grey-haired man asks charity again.
'Kind lady, I have journeyed far, and fail
    Through weariness; for I have begged in vain
Some shelter, and can find no lodging-place.' –
    She answered: 'There's the work-house very near;
    Go, for they'll certainly receive you there' –
Then shut the door against his pleading face.

Who standeth at the gate? – A stunted child,
    Her sunk eyes sharpened with precocious care.
'O lady, save me from a home defiled,
    From shameful sights and sounds that taint the air:
Take pity on me, teach me something good.' –
    'For shame, why don't you work instead of cry?
    I keep no young impostors here, not I.'
She slammed the door, indignant where she stood.

Who standeth at the gate, and will be heard?
  Arise, O woman, from thy comforts now:
Go forth again to speak the careless word,
  The cruel word unjust, with hardened brow.
But who is this, that standeth not to pray
  As once, but terrible to judge thy sin?
This whom thou wouldst not succour nor take in
Nor teach but leave to perish by the way.

'Thou didst it not unto the least of these,
  And in them hast not done it unto Me.
Thou wast as a princess rich and at ease –
  Now sit in dust and howl for poverty.
Three times I stood beseeching at thy gate,
  Three times I came to bless thy soul and save:
  But now I come to judge for what I gave,
And now at length thy sorrow is too late.'

Resurrection Eve

He resteth: weep not;
The living sleep not
With so much calm.
  He hears no chiding
  And no deriding,
  Hath joy for sorrow,
  For night hath morrow,
For wounds hath balm,
For life's strange riot
Hath death and quiet.
Who would recall him
  Of those that love him?
No fears appall him,
No ills befall him;
  There's nought above him
Save turf and flowers

And pleasant grass.
Pass the swift hours,
    How swiftly pass!
The hours of slumber
He doth not number;
Grey hours of morning
Ere the day's dawning;
Brightened by gleams
Of the sunbeams –
By the foreseeing
    Of resurrection,
    Of glorious being,
    Of full perfection,
    Of sins forgiven
        Before the face
            Of men and spirits;
    Of God in heaven,
        The resting-place
        That he inherits.

If Only

If only I might love my God and die! –
    But now He bids me love Him and live on,
    Now when the bloom of all my life is gone,
The pleasant half of life has quite gone by.
My tree of hope is lopt that spread so high;
    And I forget how summer glowed and shone,
    While autumn grips me with its fingers wan,
And frets me with its fitful windy sigh.
When autumn passes then must winter numb,
    And winter may not pass a weary while.
    But when it passes spring shall flower again:
And in that spring who weepeth now shall smile –
    Yea, they shall wax who now are on the wane,
Yea, they shall sing for love when Christ shall come.

CELIA THAXTER
1835–1894

Celia Thaxter was brought up on a lighthouse island ten miles off the New Hampshire coast, in the Isles of Shoals. That early experience gave her a lasting love of and fear of the sea, a theme that appears constantly in her poetry. Her father became a lighthouse keeper when she was four, and she, her parents and two brothers were the sole inhabitants of the island for many years. In 1841, they moved to another of the islands, Smutty Nose, where they took in paying guests. Thomas Laighton, Celia's father, then began to build a resort hotel on Appledore Island. He completed it with Levi Lincoln Thaxter, a young Harvard graduate employed to be Celia's tutor, in 1848, and the house became a major attraction every summer, luring New England writers such as Hawthorne, Lowell, Emerson and Whittier.

Many of the writers were as attracted by Celia as they were by the scenery and the hotel, and she began a literary salon of a kind in the 1860s. She and Levi Thaxter were married in 1851. They had three sons, but the marriage was not happy and Celia, living on the Massachusetts mainland, pined for Appledore. By the end of the 1860s the couple lived largely apart, though they never divorced, and Celia remained on Appledore with her mother and her eldest son Karl, who was mentally handicapped.

In 1877 Mrs Laighton died, an event which produced a kind of religious crisis in Celia's life. She tried to communicate with her mother through seances and, after an atheistic or agnostic early life, turned increasingly to theosophy, spiritualism and the religions of the east. Her poetry reflects that, but most of all it carries a note of harshness, almost bitterness, about nature as she perceived it, and about the life she lived.

The Sandpiper

Across the narrow beach we flit,
    One little sandpiper and I;
And fast I gather, bit by bit,
    The scattered driftwood bleached and dry.
The wild waves reach their hands for it,
    The wild wind raves, the tide runs high,
As up and down the beach we flit –
    One little sandpiper and I.

Above our heads the sullen clouds
    Scud black and swift across the sky:
Like silent ghosts in misty shrouds
    Stand out the white light-houses high.
Almost as far as eye can reach
    I see the close-reefed vessels fly,
As fast we flit along the beach –
    One little sandpiper and I.

I watch him as he skims along,
    Uttering his sweet and mournful cry.
He starts not at my fitful song,
    Or flash of fluttering drapery.
He has no thought of any wrong:
    He scans me with a fearless eye:
Staunch friends are we, well tried and strong,
    The little sandpiper and I.

Comrade, where wilt thou be to-night
    When the loosed storm breaks furiously?
My driftwood fire will burn so bright!
    To what warm shelter canst thou fly?
I do not fear for thee, though wroth
    The tempest rushes through the sky:
For are we not God's children both,
    Thou, little sandpiper, and I?

LOUISE CHANDLER MOULTON
1835–1908

Louise Chandler Moulton was born on a farm outside the town in Connecticut settled by her Puritan ancestors. Her parents were wealthy Calvinists, and she had a happy but limited childhood. She first published poems at the age of fifteen, and when she went to school at Emma Willard's Female Academy at Troy, New York, she was known by her fellow students as the author of *This, That and the Other* and the editor of *The Book of the Boudoir*. In 1855 she married William Moulton, editor of *The True Flag*, a Boston literary journal. They lived in the foremost literary and intellectual circles of the day, and Louise gradually wrote more and more, becoming the Boston literary correspondent for the *New York Tribune* in 1870, and contributing to ever more popular and famous journals and magazines. She first went to Europe in 1876, and so loved it that she kept on returning, living her life on both sides of the Atlantic thereafter. She was hugely successful in London, and was introduced to everyone on the literary scene.

There is in her poetry a real concern about death and clear spiritual searching. Her themes were largely love and death, about which she used to joke, half-ruefully. But she certainly meditated upon death's meaning in some of her verse, particularly as she grew older.

The House of Death

Not a hand has lifted the latchet
　　Since she went out of the door –
No footstep shall cross the threshold,
　　Since she can come in no more.

There is rust upon locks and hinges,
　　And mould and blight on the walls,
And silence faints in the chambers,
　　And darkness waits in the halls –

Waits as all things have waited
Since she went, that day of spring,
Borne in her pallid splendor
To dwell in the Court of the King.

The birds make insolent music
Where the sunshine riots outside,
And the winds are merry and wanton
With the summer's pomp and pride.

But into this desolate mansion
Where love has closed the door,
Nor sunshine nor summer shall enter,
Since she can come in no more.

ELLEN MARY CLERKE
1840–1906

Ellen Mary Clarke was born in Skibbereen, County Cork. Her father
was a bank manager and classical scholar, and her mother's family, the
Deasys, were well known locally. She was educated at home, and then
travelled in Europe with her family from 1867 to 1876. An accomp-
lished linguist, she studied Arabic and Italian literature, and wrote
regularly for the *Tablet* and the *Westminster Review*. She published a
volume of poetry, *The Flying Dutchman and Other Poems* (1881), as
well as monographs and large numbers of articles. Her sister and
constant companion was Agnes Mary Clerke, a well-known astrono-
mer, and Ellen learned some astronomy as a result. She also wrote a
novel, *Flowers of Fire*, about spies and revolutionaries, and published
a large number of translations of other writers' works. Her poetry has
been subject to a lot of criticism, but she certainly wrote in an
accomplished style, even if the content is not always to today's taste.

The Building and Pinnacle of the Temple

Not made with hands, its walls began to climb
From roots in Life's foundations deeply set,
Far down amid primaeval forms, where yet
Creation's Finger seemed to grope in slime.
Yet not in vain passed those first-born of Time,
Since each some presage gave of structure met
In higher types, lest these the bond forget
That links Earth's latest to the fore-world's prime
And living stone on living stone was laid,
In scale ascending ever, grade on grade,
To that which in its Maker's eyes seemed good –
The Human Form: and in that shrine of thought,
By the long travail of the ages wrought,
The Temple of the Incarnation stood.

Through all the ages since the primal ray,
Herald of life, first smote the abysmal night
Of elemental Chaos, and the might
Of the Creative Spark informed the clay,
From worm to brute, from brute to man – its way
The Shaping Thought took upward, flight on flight,
By stages which Earth's loftiest unite
Unto her least, made kin to such as they.
As living link, or prophecy, or type
Of purpose for fulfilment yet unripe,
Each has its niche in the supreme design;
Converging to one Pinnacle, whereat
Sole stands Creation's Masterpiece – and that
Which was through her – the Human made Divine.

HARRIET ELEANOR HAMILTON-KING
1840–1920

Harriet Eleanor Hamilton-King was the daughter of Lady Harriet and Admiral William Alexander Baillie Hamilton. In 1857, aged seventeen, she read Farini's *History of the Roman State*, and that initiated her enthusiasm for Italian nationalism and her personal devotion to the Italian patriot Mazzini, with whom she corresponded from 1862 until his death ten years later. At the age of eighteen she began work on an apologia for Felice Orsini, the would-be assassin of Napoleon III, which she thought her finest poem. It was first published privately by the banker and publisher Henry Samuel King, whom she married in 1863, but appeared in 1869 in her collection *Aspromonte and Other Poems*, the title poem of which was published in the *Observer* in 1862 as 'Garibaldi at Varignano'.

She wrote 'The Disciples' after Mazzini's death, celebrating the heroic self-sacrifice of four of his followers. It was extremely popular, circulated in hospitals and other public places, and loved by Cardinal Manning, to whom she dedicated 'The Prophecy of Westminster'.

Harriet's husband died in 1878, leaving her with seven children. She continued to write despite the strain, and produced *A Book of Dreams* in 1883, and many articles and letters. Her *Letters and Recollections of Mazzini* was edited by G. M. Trevelyan in 1912, but she was by then too ill to see the book through the press. It was her relationship with Mazzini which made her famous, and her poetry is now largely forgotten, a fate it does not deserve.

From 'The Disciples'

We suffer. Why we suffer – that is hid
With God's foreknowledge in the clouds of Heaven.
The first book written sends that human cry
Out of the clear Chaldean pasture-lands
Down forty centuries; and no answer yet
Is found, nor will be found, while yet we live

In limitations of Humanity.
But yet one thought has often stayed by me
In the night-watches, which has brought at least
The patience for the hour, and made the pain
No more a burden which I groaned to leave,
But something precious which I feared to lose.
– How shall I show it, but by parables?

The sculptor, with his Psyche's wings half-hewn
May close his eyes in weariness, and wake
To meet the white cold clay of his ideal
Flushed into beating life, and singing down
The ways of Paradise. The husbandman
May leave the golden fruitage of his groves
Ungarnered, and upon the Tree of Life
Will find a richer harvest waiting him.
The soldier dying thinks upon his bride,
And knows his arms shall never clasp her more,
Until he first the face of his unborn child
Behold in heaven: for each and all of life,
In every phase of action, love, and joy,
There is fulfilment only otherwhere.

But if, impatient, thou let slip thy cross,
Thou wilt not find it in this world again,
Nor in another; here, and here alone
Is given thee to suffer for God's sake.
In other worlds we shall more perfectly
Serve Him and love Him, praise Him, work for Him,
Grow near and nearer Him with all delight;
But then we shall not any more be called
To suffer, which is our appointment here.
Canst thou not suffer then one hour, – or two?
If He should call thee from thy cross to-day,
Saying, It is finished! – that hard cross of thine
From which thou prayest for deliverance,
Thinkest thou not some passion of regret

Would overcome thee? Thou wouldst say, 'So soon?
Let me go back, and suffer yet awhile
More patiently; – I have not yet praised God.'
And He might answer to thee, – 'Never more.
All pain is done with.' Whensoe'er it comes,
That summons that we look for, it will seem
Soon, yea too soon. Let us take heed in time
That God may now be glorified in us;
And while we suffer, let us set our souls
To suffer perfectly: since this alone,
The suffering, which is this world's special grace,
May here be perfected and left behind.

– But in obedience and humility; –
Waiting on God's hand, not forestalling it.
Seek not to snatch presumptuously the palm
By self-election; poison not thy wine
With bitter herbs if He has made it sweet;
Nor rob God's treasuries because the key
Is easy to be turned by mortal hands.
The gifts of birth, death, genius, suffering,
Are all for His hand only to bestow.
Receive thy portion, and be satisfied.
Who crowns himself a king is not the more
Royal; nor he who mars himself with stripes
The more partaker of the Cross of Christ.

But if Himself He come to thee, and stand
Beside thee, gazing down on thee with eyes
That smile, and suffer; that will smite thy heart,
With their own pity, to a passionate peace;
And reach to thee Himself the Holy Cup
(With all its wreathen stems of passion-flowers
And quivering sparkles of the ruby stars),
Pallid and royal, saying 'Drink with Me';
Wilt thou refuse? Nay, not for Paradise!
The pale brow will compel thee, the pure hands

Will minister unto thee; thou shalt take
Of that communion through the solemn depths
Of the dark waters of thine agony,
With heart that praises Him, that yearns to Him
The closer through that hour. Hold fast His hand,
Though the nails pierce thine too! take only care
Lest one drop of the sacramental wine
Be spilled, of that which ever shall unite
Thee, soul and body to thy living Lord!

Therefore gird up thyself, and come, to stand
Unflinching under the unfaltering hand,
That waits to prove thee to the uttermost.
It were not hard to suffer by His hand,
If thou couldst see His face; – but in the dark!
That is the one last trial: – be it so.
Christ was forsaken, so must thou be too:
How couldst thou suffer but in seeming, else?
Thou wilt not see the face nor feel the hand,
Only the cruel crushing of the feet,
When through the bitter night the Lord comes down
To tread the winepress – Not by sight, but faith,
Endure, endure – be faithful to the end!

SARAH WILLIAMS
1841–1868

Sarah Williams was the only child of Louise and Robert Williams, who
were of Welsh extraction. She saw that as the source of her 'bardic' gift.
She was educated first at home by governesses and later at Queens
College, Harley Street, London. Since her family was wealthy, she used

the money she made from her writing for philanthropic purposes. She never enjoyed good health, and died shortly after her father, as the result of an operation. Her poetry was much admired in its time, and was published in a posthumous volume with a memoir by one of her teachers, E. H. Plumptre.

Deep-Sea Soundings

Mariner, what of the deep?
                This of the deep:
Twilight is there, and solemn, changeless calm;
Beauty is there, and tender healing balm –
Balm with no root in earth, or air, or sea,
Poised by the finger of God, it floateth free,
And, as it threads the waves, the sound doth rise –
Hither shall come no further sacrifice;
Never again the anguished clutch at life,
Never again great Love and Death in strife;
He who hath suffered all, need fear no more,
Quiet his portion now, for evermore.

Mariner, what of the deep?
                This of the deep:
Solitude dwells not there, though silence reign;
Mighty the brotherhood of loss and pain;
There is communion past the need of speech,
There is a love no words of love can reach;
Heavy the waves that superincumbent press,
But as we labour here with constant stress,
Hand doth hold out to hand not help alone,
But the deep bliss of being fully known.
There are no kindred like the kin of sorrow,
There is no hope like theirs who fear no morrow.

Mariner, what of the deep?
         This of the deep:
Though we have travelled past the line of day,
Glory of night doth light us on our way,
Radiance that comes we know not how nor whence,
Rainbows without the rain, past duller sense,
Music of hidden reefs and waves long past,
Thunderous organ tones from far-off blast,
Harmony, victrix, throned in state sublime,
Couched on the wrecks be-gemmed with pearls of time;
Never a wreck but brings some beauty here;
Down where the waves are stilled the sea shines clear;
Deeper than life the plan of life doth lie,
He who knows all, fears naught. Great Death shall die.

MAY RILEY SMITH
1842–1927

May Louise Riley was born in Rochester, New York. She became a
popular and prolific poet in middle age, and had a series of volumes
published from 1882 onwards. These included *A Gift of Gentians and
Other Verses* (1882), *The Inn of Rest* (1888), *Cradle and Armchair*
(1893) and *Sometime and Other Poems* in the same year.

The Child in Me

She follows me about My House of Life
    (This happy little ghost of my dead youth!)
She has no part in Time's relentless strife,
    She keeps her old simplicity and truth
      And laughs at grim mortality –
      This deathless child that stays with me –
This happy little ghost of my dead youth!

My House of Life is weather-stained with years –
(O Child in Me, I wonder why you stay).
Its windows are bedimmed with rain of tears,
    Its walls have lost their rose – its thatch is gray:
        One after one its guests depart –
        So dull a host is my old heart –
    O Child in Me, I wonder why *You* stay!

For jealous Age whose face I would forget
    Pulls the bright flower you give me from my hair
And powders it with snow – and yet – and yet –
    I love your dancing feet and jocund air,
        And have no taste for caps of lace
        To tie about my faded face:
    I love to wear *your* flower in my hair!

O Child in Me, leave not My House of Clay
    Until we pass together through its door!
When lights are out, and Life has gone away,
    And we depart to come again no more,
        We comrades, who have traveled far,
        Will hail the twilight and the Star
    And gladly pass together through the Door!

ALICE MEYNELL
1847–1922

Alice Meynell grew up in an artistic household in Italy where her
mother painted sunsets and her father devoted himself to his children's
education. She became a Catholic very young, and as a poet modelled
herself on Elizabeth Barrett Browning and Christina Rossetti. Wilfrid
Meynell read her sonnets and asked for an introduction. They were

married in 1877 after a short engagement and had eight children.

For many of these years of happy marriage Alice Meynell wrote very little. She became more and more occupied with issues of social justice and with bringing up her large family. She rescued the poet Francis Thompson from poverty, breaking him of his opium addiction, and subsequently cared for him all his life. She became involved in the women's suffrage campaign, in the improvement of conditions in the London slums and in the prevention of cruelty to animals. At this time much of her writing might have been anonymous, as she helped her husband first with the *Pen* and then with the *Weekly Register*. But her named writing began again in her later years, and she contributed a weekly column to the *Pall Mall Gazette*, as well as enjoying a final poetic period from the First World War until her death.

Alice Meynell's religious and spiritual themes are obvious, as is her concern with the position of women. What is less obvious, but fascinating, is her use of Italian Catholic rather than English imagery, and her reminiscences of a happy girlhood in Italy, in a family which had encouraged her creativity, and let her experiment with her own religious ideas.

'Soeur Monique'

A Rondeau by Couperin

Quiet form of silent nun,
What has given you to my inward eyes?
What has marked you, unknown one,
In the throngs of centuries
That mine ears do listen through?
This old master's melody
That expresses you;
This admired simplicity,
Tender, with a serious wit;
And two words, the name of it,
        'Soeur Monique'.

And if sad the music is,
It is sad with mysteries
Of a small immortal thing
That the passing ages sing –
Simple music making mirth
Of the dying and the birth
Of the people of the earth.

No, not sad; we are beguiled,
Sad with living as we are;
Ours the sorrow, outpouring
Sad self on a selfless thing,
As our eyes and hearts are mild
With our sympathy for Spring,
With a pity sweet and wild
For the innocent and far,
With our sadness in a star,
Or our sadness in a child.

But two words, and this sweet air.
        Soeur Monique,
Had he more, who set you there?
Was his music-dream of you
Of some perfect nun he knew,
Or of some ideal, as true?

And I see you where you stand
With your life held in your hand
As a rosary of days.
And your thoughts in calm arrays,
And your innocent prayers are told
On your rosary of days.
And the young days and the old
With their quiet prayers did meet
When the chaplet was complete.

Did it vex you, the surmise
Of this wind of words, this storm of cries,
  Though you kept the silence so
  In the storms of long ago,
  And you keep it, like a star?
  – Of the evils triumphing,
Strong, for all your perfect conquering,
  Silenced conqueror that you are?

And I wonder at your peace, I wonder.
Would it trouble you to know,
Tender soul, the world and sin
By your calm feet trodden under
    Long ago,
Living now, mighty to win?
And your feet are vanished like the snow.

Vanished; but the poet, he
In whose dream your face appears,
He who ranges unknown years
With your music in his heart,
Speaks to you familiarly
Where you keep apart,
And invents you as you were.
And your picture, O my nun!
Is a strangely easy one,
For the holy weed you wear,
For your hidden eyes and hidden hair,
And in picturing you I may
Scarcely go astray.

O the vague reality,
The mysterious certainty!
O strange truth of these my guesses
In the wide thought-wildernesses!
– Truth of one divined of many flowers;
Of one raindrop in the showers

Of the long ago swift rain;
Of one tear of many tears
In some world-renownèd pain;
Of one daisy 'mid the centuries of sun;
Of a little living nun
In the garden of the years.

Yes, I am not far astray;
But I guess you as might one
Pausing when young March is grey,
In a violet-peopled day;
All his thoughts go out to places that he knew,
To his child-home in the sun,
To the fields of his regret,
To one place i' the innocent March air,
By one olive, and invent
The familiar form and scent
Safely; a white violet
Certainly is there.

Soeur Monique, remember me.
'Tis not in the past alone
I am picturing you to be;
But my little friend, my own,
In my moment, pray for me.
For another dream is mine,
And another dream is true,
    Sweeter even,
Of the little ones that shine
Lost within the light divine –
Of some meekest flower, or you,
    In the fields of heaven.

'I am the Way'

Thou art the Way.
Hadst Thou been nothing but the goal,
    I cannot say
If Thou hadst ever met my soul.

I cannot see –
I, child of process – if there lies
    An end for me,
Full of repose, full of replies.

I'll not reproach
The road that winds, my feet that err.
    Access, Approach
Art Thou, Time, Way, and Wayfarer.

Saint Catherine of Siena

Written for Strephon, who said that a woman must lean, or she should
not have his chivalry.

The light young man who was to die,
    Stopped in his frolic by the State,
Aghast, beheld the world go by;
    But Catherine crossed his dungeon gate.

She found his lyric courage dumb,
    His stripling beauties strewn in wrecks,
His modish bravery overcome;
    Small profit had he of his sex.

On any old wife's level he,
    For once – for all. But he alone –
Man – must not fear the mystery,
    The pang, the passage, the unknown:

Death. He did fear it, in his cell,
   Darkling amid the Tuscan sun;
And, weeping, at her feet he fell,
   The sacred, young, provincial nun.

She prayed, she preached him innocent;
   She gave him to the Sacrificed;
On her courageous breast he leant,
   The breast where beat the heart of Christ.

He left it for the block, with cries
   Of victory on his severed breath.
That crimson head she clasped, her eyes
   Blind with the splendour of his death.

And will the man of modern years
   – Stern on the Vote – withhold from thee,
Thou prop, thou cross, erect, in tears,
   Catherine, the service of his knee?

Veni Creator

So humble things Thou hast borne for us, O God,
Left'st Thou a path of lowliness untrod?
Yes, one, till now; another Olive-Garden.
For we endure the tender pain of pardon –
One with another we forbear. Give heed,
Look at the mournful world Thou hast decreed.
The time has come. At last we hapless men
Know all our haplessness all through. Come, then,
Endure undreamed humility: Lord of Heaven,
Come to our ignorant hearts and be forgiven.

Via, et Veritas, et Vita

'You never attained to Him?' 'If to attain
    Be to abide, then that may be.'
'Endless the way, followed with how much pain!'
    'The way was He.'

Beyond Knowledge

'Your sins . . . shall be white as snow.'

Into the rescued world newcomer,
    The newly-dead stepped up, and cried,
'O what is that, sweeter than summer
    Was to my heart before I died?
Sir (to an angel), what is yonder
    More bright than the remembered skies,
A lovelier sight, a softer splendour
    Than when the moon was wont to rise?
Surely no sinner wears such seeming
    Even the Rescued World within?'

'O the success of His redeeming!
    O child, it is a rescued sin!'

The Lord's Prayer

'Audemus dicere "Pater Noster".' – CANON OF THE MASS

There is a bolder way,
There is a wilder enterprise than this
All-human iteration day by day.
Courage, mankind! Restore Him what is His.

Out of His mouth were given
These phrases. O replace them whence they came.
He, only, knows our inconceivable 'Heaven',
Our hidden 'Father', and the unspoken 'Name';

Our 'trespasses', our 'bread',
The 'will' inexorable yet implored;
The miracle-words that are and are not said,
Charged with the unknown purpose of their Lord.

'Forgive', 'give', 'lead us not' –
Speak them by Him, O man the unaware,
Speak by that dear tongue, though thou know not what,
Shuddering through the paradox of prayer.

Intimations of Mortality

From Recollections of Early Childhood

A simple child . . .
That lightly draws its breath
And feels its life in every limb,
What should it know of death?
WORDSWORTH

It knows but will not tell.
Awake, alone, it counts its father's years –
How few are left – its mother's. Ah, how well
It knows of death, in tears.

If any of the three –
Parents and child – believe they have prevailed
To keep the secret of mortality,
I know that two have failed.

The third, the lonely, keeps
   One secret – a child's knowledge. When they come
At night to ask wherefore the sweet one weeps,
   Those hidden lips are dumb.

Christ in the Universe

With this ambiguous earth
His dealings have been told us. These abide:
The signal to a maid, the human birth,
The lesson, and the young Man crucified.

   But not a star of all
The innumerable host of stars has heard
How He administered this terrestrial ball.
Our race have kept their Lord's entrusted Word.

   Of His earth-visiting feet
None knows the secret, cherished, perilous,
The terrible, shamefast, frightened, whispered, sweet,
Heart-shattering secret of His way with us.

   No planet knows that this
Our wayside planet, carrying land and wave,
Love and life multiplied, and pain and bliss,
Bears, as chief treasure, one forsaken grave.

   Nor, in our little day,
May His devices with the heavens be guessed,
His pilgrimage to thread the Milky Way,
Or His bestowals there be manifest.

   But, in the eternities,
Doubtless we shall compare together, hear
A million alien Gospels, in what guise
He trod the Pleiades, the Lyre, the Bear.

O be prepared, my soul!
To read the inconceivable, to scan
The million forms of God those stars unroll
When, in our turn, we show to them a Man.

To the Mother of Christ the Son of Man

We too (one cried)), we too,
We the unready, the perplexed, the cold,
Must shape the Eternal in our thoughts anew,
    Cherish, possess, enfold.

Thou sweetly, we in strife.
It is our passion to conceive Him thus
In mind, in sense, within our house of life;
    That seed is locked in us.

We must affirm our Son
From the ambiguous Nature's difficult speech,
Gather in darkness that resplendent One,
    Close as our grasp can reach.

Nor shall we ever rest
From this our task. An hour sufficed for thee,
Thou innocent! He lingers in the breast
    Of our humanity.

EMMA LAZARUS
1849–1887

Emma Lazarus was born into a Sephardic Jewish family in New York and began writing poetry in her teenage years. Reports of the first of the terrible pogroms in Russia in 1881 inspired her with the cause of Jewish national revival, and her work on Ward's Island (later Ellis Island) amongst the Russian Jewish refugees convinced her of the need for a Jewish national home.

She continued to work as a defender of the twin homelands for the Jews of the Holy Land and the United States, but it is for the sonnet she wrote about the States as the haven for Europe's 'huddled masses yearning to breathe free' that she is most remembered. It was affixed to the base of the Statue of Liberty in 1903. After her death, her sister would not allow anything of Jewish interest which she had written to be included in the collected edition of her works which appeared in 1889.

The Banner of the Jew

Wake, Israel wake! Recall to-day
   The glorious Maccabean rage,
The sire heroic, hoary-grey,
   His five-fold lion-lineage:
The Wise, the Elect, the Help-of-God,
The Burst-of-Spring, the Avenging Rod.

From Mizpeh's mountain-ridge they saw
   Jerusalem's empty streets, her shrine
Laid waste where Greeks profaned the Law,
   With idol and with pagan sign.
Mourners in tattered black were there,
With ashes sprinkled on their hair.

Then from the stony peak there rang
   A blast to ope the graves; down poured
The Maccabean clan, who sang
   Their battle-anthem to the Lord.
Five heroes lead, and following, see,
Ten thousand rush to Victory!

Oh for Jerusalem's trumpet now,
   To blow a blast of shattering power,
To wake the sleepers high and low,
   And rouse them to the urgent hour!
No hand for vengeance – but to save,
A million naked swords should wave.

Oh deem not dead that martial fire,
   Say not the mystic flame is spent!
With Moses' law and David's lyre,
   Your ancient strength remains unbent.
Let but an Ezra rise anew,
To lift the *Banner of the Jew.*

A rag, a mock at first – erelong,
   When men have bled, and women wept
To guard its precious folds from wrong,
   Even they who shrunk, even they who slept,
Shall leap to bless it, and to save.
Strike! for the brave revere the brave!

The New Colossus

Not like the brazen giant of Greek fame,
With conquering limbs astride from land to land;
Here at our sea-washed, sunset gates shall stand
A mighty woman with a torch, whose flame
Is the imprisoned lightning, and her name
Mother of Exiles. From her beacon-hand

Glows world-wide welcome; her mild eyes command
The air-bridged harbor that twin cities frame.
'Keep, ancient lands, your storied pomp!' cries she
With silent lips. 'Give me your tired, your poor,
Your huddled masses yearning to breathe free,
The wretched refuse of your teeming shore.
Send these, the homeless, tempest-tost to me,
I lift my lamp beside the golden door!'

ELLA WHEELER WILCOX
1850–1919

Ella Wheeler Wilcox produced an eleven-chapter 'novel' when she was
nine, and continued to write, embarking on an active literary career
when the family subscription to the *New York Mercury* ran out and she
submitted some sketches which enabled the subscription to be
reinstated. In 1872 she responded to the temperance promotion of the
Good Templars with a volume of poems, *Drops of Water*, which
received some public acclamation. She followed that with *Shells*, a
volume of positive and optimistic religious verse not dissimilar in style
to much of her later work. By her writing, she was helping to support
the family, and this included the families of her elder brothers and sister
who had failed at farming.

As she became more famous, she was hired by a Milwaukee firm to
write a column for its trade journal. After that, she reached real
distinction when a Chicago publishing firm refused to publish her more
emotional love poems, saying they were immoral! The poems were not
sensational, but it was the title, *Poems of Passion*, that offended mid-
Victorian American sensibilities. Another Chicago publisher saw a
commercial advantage in the ensuing row, in which the poems were
described as seeming to 'out-Swinburne Swinburne and out-Whitman
Whitman'. Sixty thousand copies were sold in the first two years, and
her fortune was made – as well as her reputation.

Her poetry is not really very good, but it clearly touched the hearts and minds of literally millions of people. She was no minor poet. Instead, she was a poor quality poet of major significance, whose record has to be studied carefully, and who hit a public nerve better poets failed to capture at all.

Laugh, and the World Laughs With You

Laugh, and the world laughs with you;
    Weep, and you weep alone;
For this brave old earth must borrow its mirth,
    It has trouble enough of its own.
Sing, and the hills will answer;
    Sigh! it is lost on the air;
The echoes bound to a joyful sound,
    But shrink from voicing care.

Rejoice, and men will seek you;
    Grieve, and they turn and go;
They want full measure of all your pleasure,
    But they do not want your woe.
Be glad, and your friends are many;
    Be sad, and you lose them all –
There are none to decline your nectared wine,
    But alone you must drink life's gall.

Feast, and your halls are crowded;
    Fast, and the world goes by.
Succeed and give, and it helps you live,
    But no man can help you die.
There is room in the halls of pleasure
    For a long and lordly train:
But one by one we must all file on
    Through the narrow aisles of pain.

EDITH M. THOMAS
1854–1925

Edith Thomas was born in Ohio in 1854. The family moved from place to place; Edith's father died in 1862 and she went to public school in Geneva, Ohio. In 1872, she worked for two terms as a teacher, and then turned to literature as a career. She wrote for a number of newspapers, and Helen Hunt Jackson (whose work is included elsewhere in this volume) welcomed her as a colleague writing for the *Century* and the *Atlantic Monthly*. Edith published several highly respected volumes of poetry, including *The Inverted Torch* (1890), *In Sunshine Lane* (1895) and *The Flower from the Ashes* (1915).

Spirit to Spirit

Dead? Not to thee, thou keen watcher – not silent, not viewless, to thee,
Immortal still wrapped in the mortal! I, from the mortal set free,
Greet thee by many clear tokens thou smilest to hear and to see.

For I, when thou wakest at dawn, to thee am the entering morn;
And I, when thou walkest abroad, am the dew on the leaf and the thorn,
The tremulous glow of the noon, the twilight on harvests of corn.

I am the flower by the wood-path – thou bendest to look in my eyes;
The bird in its nest in the thicket – thou heedest my love-laden cries;
The planet that leads the night legions, – thou liftest thy gaze to the
  skies.

And I am the soft-dropping rain, the snow with its fluttering swarms;
The summer-day cloud on the hilltops, that showeth thee manifold
  forms;
The wind from the south and the west, the voice that sings courage in
  storms!

Sweet was the earth to thee ever, but sweeter by far to thee now:
How hast thou room for tears, when all times marvelest thou,
Beholding who dwells with God in the blossoming sward and the
    bough!

Once as a wall were the mountains, once darkened between us the sea;
No longer these thwart and baffle, forbidding my passage to thee:
Immortal still wrapped in the mortal, I linger till thou art set free!

The Courage of the Lost

There be those who are afraid to fear,
    The myrmidons of Hope!
Their watchword cannot lend me cheer
    'Gainst that with which I cope!

There is a courage of the lost,
    Who sail uncharted seas,
Past many a firm, or flying coast,
    And I must sail with these.

There is a valor of the slain,
    Who strive past mortal sight
While their spent corses strew the plain,
    And I must fight their fight.

Hast thou that courage of the lost,
    Past theirs that reach their goal?
Whoever thou art, I thee accost –
    Thou Comrade of my Soul!

Thou dost not fear to fear – ah, no!
    The depths wilt thou descend;
And when thy planet sinketh low
    Wilt make of Night a friend!

Then come! We two are proof, at last,
We dare our fears to own;
But had our lot with Hope been cast
What heart-break had we known!

SARAH PRATT MCLEAN GREENE
1856–1935

Born to a Bostonian family, Sarah Pratt McLean Greene taught at
Cedarville, Massachusetts, on Cape Cod and was fascinated by the
eccentricities and foreign quality of Cape Cod life; she began to publish
some of what she saw, encouraged by members of her family who had
received extremely vivid letters.

Her first novel, *Cape Cod Folks*, made her reputation, but the realism
of her accounts brought lawsuits in tow, and some damages were
awarded against her. Nevertheless, the book continued to make a large
profit, and she became better and better known. She produced more in
the same vein, but she also wrote some poetry, and a few novels set in
the west, which were much less successful. It was New England, and
particularly the Cape, which set her off, and she depicted the manners
of her New England country neighbours with devastating accuracy.
Her poetry, with its deliberate, mannered Cape Cod dialect, is hard to
read. But it betrays a strongly sensitive and spiritual person.

De Massa ob de Sheepfol'

De massa ob de sheepfol'
    Dat guards de sheepfol' bin,
Look out in de gloomerin' meadows
    Wha'r de long night rain begin –
So he call to de hirelin' shepha'd:
    'Is my sheep – is dey all come in?
    My sheep, is dey all come in?'

Oh den says de hirelin' shepha'd,
    'Dey's some, dey's black and thin,
And some, dey's po' ol' wedda's –
    Dat can't come home agin.
Dey's some black sheep an' ol' wedda's,
    But de res', dey's all brung in –
    De rest', dey's all brung in.'

Den de massa ob de sheepfol'
    Dat guards de sheepfol' bin,
Goes down in de gloomerin' meadows
    Wha'r de long night rain begin –
So he le' down de ba's ob de sheepfol',
    Callin' sof': 'Come in! Come in!'
    Callin' sof': 'Come in! Come in!'

Den up t'ro' de gloomerin' meadows,
    T'ro' de col' night rain an win',
And up t'ro' de gloomerin' rain-paf'
    Whar de sleet fa' piercin' thin,
De po' los' sheep ob de sheepfol',
    Dey all comes gadderin' in.
De po' los' sheep ob de sheepfol',
    Dey all comes gadderin' in!

LIZETTE WOODWORTH REESE
1856–1935

Lizette Woodworth Reese was born in the suburbs of Baltimore, Maryland. She first published a poem 'The Deserted House', in 1874, and she continued to write for the rest of her life. Her first volume of verse brought her fame beyond Baltimore, and second and further volumes were published by the well-known and respected publishers Houghton Mifflin. Thomas Bird Mosher acquired the rights to her work and published them in limited editions; in 1909 he published a first edition of her book *A Wayside Lute*. After this there was a long silence before Lizette began writing again in the 1920s, continuing her simple, local themes, and her account of a Maryland village in the nineteenth century. She is commemorated in Baltimore in plaques and memorials, in the places mentioned in her poems.

Tears

When I consider Life and its few years –
A wisp of fog betwixt us and the sun;
A call to battle, and the battle done
Ere the last echo dies within our ears;
A rose choked in the grass; an hour of fears;
The gusts that past a darkening shore do beat;
The burst of music down an unlistening street –
I wonder at the idleness of tears.

Ye old, old dead, and ye of yesternight,
Chieftains and bards and keepers of the sheep,
By every cup of sorrow that you had,
Loose me from tears, and make me see aright
How each hath back what once he stayed to weep:
Homer his sight, David his little lad!

Immortality

Battles nor songs can from oblivion save,
  But Fame upon a white deed loves to build;
From out that cup of water Sidney gave,
  Not one drop has been spilled.

A. MARY F. ROBINSON
1057-1944

Agnes Mary Frances Robinson was the daughter of George Robinson,
archdiaconal architect for Coventry, and Frances Sparrow. She became
a poet, biographer and critic while her sister Mabel became a novelist.
Her best known work is a collection of poems published in 1886, *An
Italian Garden*.

Pallor

The great white lilies in the grass
  Are pallid as the smile of death;
For they remember still – alas! –
  The graves they sprang from underneath.

The angels up in heaven are pale –
  For all have died, when all is said;
Nor shall the lutes of Eden avail
  To let them dream they are not dead.

E. NESBIT
1858–1924

Edith Nesbit is far better known as an author of children's books than as a poet. Indeed, the complicated and passionate side of her character is often kept hidden from the public gaze precisely because she ought to appear as the wholesome, motherly author of *The Railway Children*. Yet in truth, her life reads almost like a novel. Although she was a fine writer of children's books, she also wrote prolifically for adults, in prose and verse, and both she and her husband led stormy private lives.

   She was born in south London, in Kennington, one of four children. She married the journalist Hubert Bland and they both became ardent socialists. Hubert contracted smallpox shortly after the birth of their first child, and from then on rarely made enough money to support the family, leaving the financial questions to Edith. He ran a double life with one Margaret Doran for at least the first ten years of his marriage, and also became entangled with Edith's best friend, Alice Hoatson, whose two children by him were brought up as if they were Edith's. Edith, Hubert and Alice lived for years in a *ménage à trois* which Edith found both comforting and disturbing as she went after lovers herself – her most famous conquest was George Bernard Shaw.

   Through all this she made a living from her writing, eventually a handsome living. Her children's books were the most profitable, but her poetry and some of her other prose also began to be fashionable. However Hubert – and perhaps Edith herself – seem to have frittered money away, and after his death she was far from well off. In 1917 she married the easy-going Tommy Tucker, known as 'the Skipper' and her last years were rich in love and devotion, but short of cash and comfort.

   Edith Nesbit was an extraordinary woman. Despite her politics, her extraordinary sexual exploits and the unconventionalities of her life, she was also a profoundly believing Christian. Her second marriage took place in a Catholic church, and she was buried in the Church of England cemetery near where she and Tommy lived.

   Nowadays, only her children's books are widely read, though her poetry is beginning to reappear in anthologies, and has been vastly

underrated. It is at its most fascinating when it is not clear to whom it
is addressed.

Among His Books

A silent room – gray with a dusty blight
    Of loneliness;
A room with not enough of life or light
    Its form to dress.

Books enough though! The groaning sofa bears
    A goodly store
Books on the window-seat, and on the chairs,
    And on the floor.

Books of all sorts of soul, all sorts of age,
    All sorts of face –
Black-letter, vellum, and the flimsy page
    Of commonplace.

All bindings, from the cloth whose hue distracts
    One's weary nerves,
To yellow parchment, binding rare old tracts
    It serves – deserves.

Books on the shelves, and in the cupboard books,
    Worthless and rare –
Books on the mantelpiece – where'er one looks
    Books everywhere!

Books! books! the only things in life I find
    Not wholly vain.
Books in my hands – books in my heart enshrined –
    Books in my brain.

My friends are they: for children and for wife
    They serve me too;
For these alone, of all dear things in life,
    Have I found true.

They do not flatter, change, deny, deceive –
    Ah no – not they!
The same editions which one night you leave
    You find next day.

You don't find railway novels where you left
    Your Elzevirs!
Your Aldines don't betray you – leave bereft
    Your lonely years!

And yet this common book of Common Prayer
    My heart prefers,
Because the names upon the fly-leaf there
    Are mine and hers.

It's a dead flower that makes it open so –
    Forget-me-not –
The Marriage Service . . . well, my dear, you know
    Who first forgot.

Those were the days when in the choir we two
    Sat – used to sing –
When I believed in God, in love, in you –
    In everything.

Through quiet lanes to church we used to come,
    Happy and good,
Clasp hands through sermon, and go slowly home
    Down through the wood.

Kisses? A certain yellow rose no doubt
    That porch still shows,
Whenever I hear kisses talked about
    I smell that rose!

No – I don't blame you – since you only proved
    My choice unwise,
And taught me books should trusted be and loved,
    Not lips and eyes!

And so I keep your book – your flower – to show
    How much I care
For the dear memory of what, you know,
    You never were.

The Gray Folk

The house, with blind unhappy face,
    Stands lonely in the last year's corn,
    And in the grayness of the morn
The gray folk come about the place.

By many pathways, gliding gray
    They come past meadow, wood, and wold,
    Come by the farm and by the fold
From the green fields of yesterday.

Past lock and chain and bolt and bar
    They press, to stand about my bed,
    And like the faces of the dead
I know their hidden faces are.

They will not leave me in the day
    And when night falls they will not go,
    Because I silenced, long ago,
The only voice that they obey.

Surrender

The wild wind wails in the poplar tree,
        I sit here alone.
O heart of my heart, come hither to me!
Come to me straight over land and sea,
        My soul – my own!

Not now – the clock's slow tick I hear,
        And nothing more.
The year is dying, the leaves are sere,
No ghost of the beautiful young crowned year
        Knocks at my door.

But one of these nights, a wild, late night,
        I, waiting within,
Shall hear your hand on the latch – and spite
Of prudence and folly and wrong and right,
        I shall let you in.

The Things That Matter

Now that I've nearly done my days,
    And grown too stiff to sweep or sew,
I sit and think, till I'm amaze,
    About what lots of things I know:
Things as I've found out one by one –
    And when I'm fast down in the clay,
My knowing things and how they're done
    Will all be lost and thrown away.

There's things, I know, as won't be lost,
    Things as folks write and talk about:
The way to keep your roots from frost,
    And how to get your ink spots out.
What medicine's good for sores and sprains,

What way to salt your butter down,
What charms will cure your different pains,
   And what will bright your faded gown.

But more important things than these,
   They can't be written in a book:
How fast to boil your greens and peas,
   And how good bacon ought to look;
The feel of real good wearing stuff,
   The kind of apple as will keep,
The look of bread that's rose enough,
   And how to get a child asleep.

Whether the jam is fit to pot,
   Whether the milk is going to turn,
Whether a hen will lay or not,
   Is things as some folks never learn.
I know the weather by the sky,
   I know what herbs grow in what lane;
And if sick men are going to die,
   Of if they'll get about again.

Young wives come in, a-smiling, grave,
   With secrets that they itch to tell:
I know what sort of times they'll have,
   And if they'll have a boy or gell.
And if a lad is ill to bind,
   Or some young maid is hard to lead,
I know when you should speak 'em kind,
   And when it's scolding as they need.

I used to know where birds ud set,
   And likely spots for trout or hare,
And God may want me to forget
   The way to set a line or snare;
But not the way to truss a chick,

To fry a fish, or baste a roast,
Nor how to tell, when folks are sick,
　　What kind of herb will ease them most!

Forgetting seems such silly waste!
　　I know so many little things,
And now the Angels will make haste
　　To dust it all away with wings!
O God, you made me like to know,
　　You kept the things straight in my head,
Please God, if you can make it so,
　　Let me know *something* when I'm dead.

The Confession

I haven't always acted good:
　　I've taken things not meant for me;
Not other people's drink and food,
　　But things they never seemed to see.
I haven't done the way I ought
　　If all they say in church is true,
But all I've had I've fairly bought,
　　And paid for pretty heavy too.

For days and weeks are very long
　　If you get nothing new and bright,
And if you never do no wrong
　　Somehow you never do no right.
The chap that daresent go a yard
　　For fear the path should lead astray
May be a saint – though that seems hard,
　　But he's no traveller, any way.

Some things I can't be sorry for,
　　The things that silly people hate;
But some I did I do deplore,
　　I knew, inside, they wasn't straight.

And when my last account is filed,
  And stuck-up angels stop their song,
I'll ask God's pardon like a child
  For what I really knew was wrong.

If you've a child, you'd rather see
  A bit of temper, off and on,
A greedy grab, a silly spree –
  And then a brave thing said or done
Than hear your boy whine all day long
  About the things he mustn't do:
Just doing nothing, right or wrong:
  And God may feel the same as you.

For God's our Father, so they say,
  He made His laws and He made me;
He'll understand about the way
  Me and His laws could not agree.
He might say, 'You're worth more, My son,
  Than all My laws since law began.
Take good with bad – here's something done –
  And I'm your God, and you're My man.'

After Death

If we must part, this parting is the best:
  How would you bear to lay
  Your head on some warm pillow far away –
Your head, so used to lying on my breast?

But now your pillow is cold;
Your hands have flowers, and not my hands, to hold;
Upon our bed the worn bride-linen lies.
I have put the death-money upon your eyes,
So that you should not wake up in the night.
I have bound your face with white;

I have washed you, yes, with water and not with tears –
Those arms wherein I have slept so many years,
Those feet that hastened when they came to me,
And all your body that belonged to me.
I have smoothed your dear dull hair,
And there is nothing left to say for you
And nothing left to fear or pray for you;
And I have got the rest of life to bear:
Thank God it is you, not I, who are lying there.
If I had died
And you had stood beside
This still white bed
Where the white, scented, horrible flowers are spread –
I know the thing it is,
And I thank God that He has spared you this.
If one must bear it, thank God it was I
Who had to live and bear to see you die,
Who have to live, and bear to see you dead.

You will have nothing of it all to bear:
You will not even know that in your bed
You lie alone. You will not miss my head
Beside you on the pillow: you will rest
So soft in the grave you will not miss my breast.
But I – but I – Your pillow and your place –
And only the darkness laid against my face,
And only my anguish pressed against my side –
Thank God, thank God, that it was you who died!

KATHARINE LEE BATES
1859–1929

Katharine Lee Bates was born at Falmouth, Massachusetts, on Cape
Cod and studied at Wellesley College and Oxford University. She joined
the staff of Wellesley, where she remained until her retirement. She
never married, but dedicated herself to her students and to the study of
literature. Although she was a prolific writer, most of her work went
and goes unread. With the exception of a few memorable pieces, she is
overlooked as a poet, and remembered as an important educator of the
next generation of literary women. But much of her work is well worth
reading, especially the volume of poems entitled *Yellow Clover* (1922)
and her stories in the form of the Canterbury Tales for Children, *The
Pilgrim Ship* (1909).

Sarah Threeneedles

Boston, 1698

By the grim grace of the Puritans she had been brought
    Into their frigid meeting-house to list
Her funeral sermon before the rope ran taut.
    Soft neck that he had kissed!

Through the narrow window her dazed blue eyes could see
    The rope. Like a glittering icicle it hung
From the hoar cross-beam of the horrible gallows-tree.
    His arms about her flung!

Two captive Indians and one Guinea slave,
    Hating at heart the merciless white God,
In the stubborn ground were hacking her shallow grave.
    Sweet April path they trod!

Her shivering neighbors thrilled to the fierce discourse
　Of the minister, who thundered the dire sting
Of a sinner's death till his vehement voice went hoarse.
　She heard love's whispering.

And still she stood while the frozen communion bread,
　That the preacher broke ere he poured the chilly wine,
Rattling into the plates, her judges fed.
　Her food was more divine.

HELEN GREY CONE
1859–1934

Helen Grey Cone was educated in public schools and then at Hunter
College, New York, where she was a teacher of English literature from
1899 onwards. She wrote many poems, two of her most notable
collections being *Oberon and Puck, Verses Grave and Gay* (1885) and
One, Two, Three, Four (1889), for children. She remained unmarried,
a dedicated teacher who taught her students creative writing in a style
ahead of her time, as well as producing a great deal of work of
considerable merit herself.

Heartbreak Road

As I went up by Heartbreak Road
　Before the dawn of day,
The cold mist was all about,
　And the wet world was gray;
It seemed that never another soul
　Had walked that weary way.

But when I came to Heartbreak Hill,
   Silver touched the sea;
I knew that many and many a soul
   Was climbing close to me;
I knew I walked that weary way
   In a great company.

CHARLOTTE PERKINS STETSON GILMAN
1860–1935

Charlotte Gilman's work attacked a variety of social ills, but her main thrust was in the labour and women's movements, and she joined the Fabian socialists in the 1890s. Her most famous work of fiction is *The Yellow Wallpaper*, which was published in 1892 in the distinguished *New England Magazine* and deals with insanity in a memorable way. She published poems at the same time, and then in 1898 the work of political thought for which she is best known, *Women and Economics*, setting out her firm belief in the need for women's economic independence.

The recognition later generations have given to her ideas and social vision would undoubtedly have given her immense pleasure. Although her poetry is relatively unknown now, it received a great deal of acclaim at the time of its first publication, and deserves at least a second look.

Child Labor

No fledgling feeds the fatherbird,
   No chicken feeds the hen,
No kitten mouses for the cat –
   This glory is for men.

We are the wisest, strongest race:
 Long may our praise be sung –
The only animal alive
 That lives upon its young!

Similar Cases

There was once a little animal,
 No bigger than a fox,
And on five toes he scampered
 Over Tertiary rocks.
They called him Eohippus,
 And they called him very small,
And they thought him of no value –
 When they thought of him at all;
For the lumpish old Dinoceras
 And Coryphodon so slow
Were the heavy aristocracy
 In days of long ago.

Said the little Eohippus,
 'I am going to be a horse!
And on my middle finger-nails
 To run my earthly course!
I'm going to have a flowing tail!
 I'm going to have a mane!
I'm going to stand fourteen hands high
 On the psycozoic plain!'

The Coryphodon was horrified,
 The Dinoceras was shocked;
And they chased young Eohippus,
 But he skipped away and mocked.
Then they laughed enormous laughter,
 And they groaned enormous groans,
And they bade young Eohippus

Go view his father's bones.
Said they, 'You always were as small
  And mean, as now we see,
And that's conclusive evidence
  That you're always going to be.
What! Be a great, tall, handsome beast,
With hoofs to gallop on?
Why! You'd have to change your nature!'
  Said the Loxolophodon.
They considered him disposed of,
  And retired with gait serene;
That was the way they argued
  In 'the early Eocene.'

There was once an Anthropoidal Ape,
  Far smarter than the rest,
And everything that they could do
  He always did the best;
So they naturally disliked him,
  And they gave him shoulders cool,
And when they had to mention him
  They said he was a fool.

Cried this pretentious Ape one day,
  'I'm going to be a Man!
And stand upright, and hunt, and fight,
  And conquer all I can!
I'm going to cut down forest trees,
  To make my houses higher!
I'm going to kill the Mastodon!
  I'm going to make a fire!'

Loud screamed the Anthropoidal Apes
  With laughter wild and gay;
They tried to catch that boastful one,
  But he always got away.
So they yelled at him in chorus,

Which he minded not a whit;
And they pelted him with cocoanuts,
   Which didn't seem to hit.
And then they gave him reasons
   Which they thought of much avail,
To prove how his preposterous
   Attempt was sure to fail.
Said the sages, 'In the first place,
   The thing cannot be done!
And, second, if it *could* be,
   It would not be any fun!
And, third, and most conclusive,
   And admitting no reply,
You would have to change your nature!
   We should like to see you try!'
They chuckled then triumphantly,
   These lean and hairy shapes,
For these things passed as arguments
   With the Anthropoidal Apes.

There was once a Neolithic Man,
   An enterprising wight,
Who made his chopping implements
   Unusually bright.
Unusually clever he,
   Unusually brave,
And he drew delightful Mammoths
   On the borders of his cave.
To his Neolithic neighbors,
   Who were startled and surprised,
Said he, 'My friends, in course of time,
   We shall be civilized!
We are going to live in cities!
   We are going to fight in wars!
We are going to eat three times a day
   Without the natural cause!

We are going to turn life upside down
  About a thing called gold!
We are going to want the earth, and take
  As much as we can hold!
We are going to wear great piles of stuff
  Outside our proper skins!
We are going to have Diseases!
  And Accomplishments!! And Sins!!!'

Then they all rose up in fury
  Against their boastful friend,
For prehistoric patience
  Cometh quickly to an end.
Said one, 'This is chimerical!
  Utopian! Absurd!'
Said another, 'What a stupid life!
  Too dull, upon my word!'
Cried all, 'Before such things can come,
  You idiotic child,
You must alter Human Nature!'
  And they all sat back and smiled.
Thought they, 'An answer to that last
  It will be hard to find!'
It was a clinching argument
  To the Neolithic Mind!

HARRIET MONROE
1860–1936

Harriet Monroe became art, drama and music correspondent for the
Chicago Tribune in the late 1880s and later an established freelance
critic and reviewer. Her poetry was never widely read. But she did

succeed in establishing a small literary monthly which she persevered
with all her life, bullying and cajoling friends into supporting her, and
campaigning to get Americans to read poetry. It is her campaigning
and her record as an enthusiast for poetry that are most remembered,
but there are a few fine poems there as well.

The Shadow Child

Why do the wheels go whirring round,
   Mother, mother?
O mother, are they giants bound,
   And will they growl forever?

Yes, fiery giants underground,
   Daughter, little daughter,
Forever turn the wheels around,
   And rumble-grumble ever.

Why do I pick the threads all day,
   Mother, mother?
While sunshine children are at play?
   And must I work forever?

Yes, shadow-child; the livelong day,
   Daughter, little daughter,
Your hands must pick the threads away,
   And feel the sunshine never.

Why do the birds sing in the sun,
   Mother, mother,
If all day long I run and run,
   Run with the wheels forever?

The birds may sing till day is done,
  Daughter, little daughter,
But with the wheels your feet must run –
  Run with the wheels forever.

Why do I feel so tired each night,
  Mother, mother?
The wheels are always buzzing bright;
  Do they grow sleepy never?

O baby-thing, so soft and white,
  Daughter, little daughter,
The big wheels grind us in their might,
  And they will grind forever.

And is the white thread never spun,
  Mother, mother?
And is the white cloth never done,
  For you and me done never?

Oh, yes, our thread will all be spun,
  Daughter, little daughter,
When we lie down out in the sun,
  And work no more forever.

And when will come that happy day,
  Mother, mother?
Oh, shall we laugh and sing and play,
  Out in the sun forever?

No, shadow-child, we'll rest all day,
  Daughter, little daughter,
Where green grass grows and roses gay,
  There in the sun forever.

A Farewell

Good-by – no, do not grieve that it is over,
  The perfect hour;
That the wingèd joy, sweet honey-loving rover,
  Flits from the flower.

Grieve not – it is the law. Love will be flying –
  Oh, love and all.
Glad was the living – blessed be the dying!
  Let the leaves fall.

AMY LEVY
1861–1889

Amy Levy showed early literary talent. Some of her poems were
published while she was a student at Cambridge; in 1889 she published
her lyrical collection *A London Plane-Tree and Other Poems*, which
contains many fine, though depressing, poems.

Her most powerful literary work was a novel, *Reuben Sachs*, dealing
with the least attractive aspects of Jewish society of the time and with
the tension between Jewish and English life. But although her work
was received with pleasure, and, in the case of *Reuben Sachs*, with
acclamation, and although she disguised her unhappiness with super-
ficial gaiety, she was a deeply troubled person. She committed suicide at
her parents' home in London in 1889, as far as is known because of
depression and growing deafness.

Her work ought to appear immature, which it does not. But it is
obvious that she had far more to give, and it is a great pity that such a
great talent died so young, with so little left for us to remember her by.

A London Plane-Tree

Green is the plane-tree in the square,
  The other trees are brown;
They droop and pine for country air,
  The plane-tree loves the town.

Here from my garret-pane I mark
  The plane-tree bud and blow,
Shed her recuperative bark,
  And spread her shade below.

Among her branches, in and out,
  The city breezes play;
The dull fog wraps her round about;
  Above, the smoke curls grey.

Others the country take for choice,
  And hold the town in scorn;
But she has listen'd to the voice
  On city breezes borne.

Epitaph

On a commonplace person who died in bed

This is the end of him, here he lies:
The dust in his throat, the worm in his eyes,
The mould in his mouth, the turf on his breast;
This is the end of him, this is best.
He will never lie on his couch awake,
Wide-eyed, tearless, till dim daybreak.
Never again will he smile and smile
When his heart is breaking all the while.
He will never stretch out his hands in vain
Groping and groping – never again.

Never ask for bread, get a stone instead,
Never pretend that the stone is bread.
Never sway and sway 'twixt the false and true,
Weighing and noting the long hours through.
Never ache and ache with the chok'd-up sighs;
This is the end of him, here he lies.

On the Threshold

O God, my dream! I dreamed that you were dead;
Your mother hung above the couch and wept
Whereon you lay all white, and garlanded
With blooms of waxen whiteness. I had crept
Up to your chamber-door, which stood ajar,
And in the doorway watched you from afar,
Nor dared advance to kiss your lips and brow.
I had no part nor lot in you, as now;
Death had not broken between us the old bar;
Nor torn from out my heart the old, cold sense
Of your misprision and my impotence.

MARY ELIZABETH COLERIDGE
1861–1907

Mary Coleridge followed her great-great-uncle in her taste for the
supernatural in her poetry. Educated at home, she wrote romantic and
mystical poetry and stories. By 1881, her first essays were appearing in
a variety of periodicals, and she published her first novel, *The Seven
Sleepers of Ephesus*, in 1893. But her verse remained a secret until the
future Poet Laureate, Robert Bridges, caught a glimpse of it, became
interested in it and persuaded her to publish a volume of it in 1896. The

collection, entitled *Fancy's Following*, was printed privately. The following year she published another novel, *The King with Two Faces*, which caught the attention of a wider public.

Although she continued to produce poetry, essays and novels for the rest of her life, she spent surprisingly little of her time on writing, instead devoting great quantities of her energy to the working women of London, to whom she lectured at the Working Women's College. After her sudden death in 1907, her great admirer, Henry Newbolt, published her poems, and in 1910 there followed *Gathered Leaves*, a collection of her essays and diaries. In her poems there are signs both of her taste for the supernatural and of her social concern, but the supernatural prevails.

A Moment

The clouds had made a crimson crown
    Above the mountains high.
The stormy sun was going down
    In a stormy sky.

Why did you let your eyes so rest on me,
    And hold your breath between?
In all the ages this can never be
    As if it had not been.

Shadow

Child of my love! though thou be bright as day,
    Though all the sons of joy laugh and adore thee,
Thou canst not throw thy shadow self away.
    Where thou dost come, the earth is darker for thee.

When thou dost pass, a flower that saw the sun
  Sees him no longer.
The hosts of darkness are, thou radiant one,
  Through thee made stronger.

Unwelcome

We were young, we were merry, we were very very wise,
  And the door stood open at our feast,
When there passed us a woman with the West in her eyes,
  And a man with his back to the East.

Oh, still grew the hearts that were beating so fast,
  The loudest voice was still.
The jest died away on our lips as they passed,
  And the rays of July struck chill.

The cups of red wine turned pale on the board,
  The white bread black as soot.
The hound forgot the hand of her lord,
  She fell down at his foot.

Low let me lie, where the dead dog lies,
  Ere I sit me down again at a feast,
When there passes a woman with the West in her eyes,
  And a man with his back to the East.

'He knoweth not that the dead are thine'

The weapon that you fought with was a word,
And with that word you stabbed me to the heart.
Not once but twice you did it, for the sword
  Made no blood start.

They have not tried you for your life. You go
Strong in such innocence as men will boast.
They have not buried me. They do not know
   Life from its ghost.

Change

Ah, there is no abiding!
   Signs from heaven are sent.
Over the grass the wind went gliding,
   And the green grass grew silver as he went.

Ah, there is no remaining!
   Ever the tide of ocean ebbs and flows.
Over the blue sea goes the wind complaining,
   And the blue sea turns emerald as he goes.

Cut It Down

By a dim road, o'ergrown with dry thin grass,
   A little straggling, wild, wind-beaten tree
Stood, like a sentry, where no feet might pass,
   And storm-swept by the sea.

What was the secret of that lonely place?
   Had some accursèd thing gone by this way,
Leaving the horror of his evil face
   On leaf and bough and spray?

I know not. But the very sunbeams took
   The darkness of the gnarled and twisted stem;
The summer air those wrinkled leaves forsook
   Nor ever played in them.

On Such a Day

Some hang above the tombs,
Some weep in empty rooms,
I, when the iris blooms,
Remember.

I, when the cyclamen
Opens her buds again,
Rejoice a moment – then
Remember.

Gibberish

Many a flower have I seen blossom,
Many a bird for me will sing.
Never heard I so sweet a singer,
Never saw I so fair a thing.

She is a bird, a bird that blossoms,
She is a flower, a flower that sings;
And I a flower when I behold her,
And when I hear her, I have wings.

MADGE MORRIS WAGNER
1862–1924

Madge Wagner was born on the plains, on the way to California, as her parents were making the trek westwards. From 1885–95 she edited the *Golden Gate*, a local San Francisco journal. She was a prolific author, journalist and poet, and numbered amongst her works *Merie, Diana, A Titled Plebeian* and *The Mystery of Carmel and Other Poems*.

To the Colorado Desert

Thou brown, bare-breasted, voiceless mystery,
Hot sphynx of nature, cactus-crowned, what hast thou done?
Unclothed and mute as when the groans of chaos turned
Thy naked burning bosom to the sun.
The mountain silences have speech, the rivers sing,
Thou answerest never unto anything.
Pink throated lizards pant in thy slim shade;
The hornèd toad runs rustling in the heat;
The shadowy gray coyote, born afraid,
Steals to some brackish spring, and leaps and prowls
Away, and howls and howls and howls and howls,
Until the solitude is shaken with added loneliness.
The sharp mescal shoots up a giant stalk,
Its centuries of yearning to the sunburnt skies,
And drops rare honey from the lips
Of yellow waxen flowers, and dies.
Some lengthwise sun-dried shapes with feet and hands,
And thirsty mouths pressed on the sweltering sands,
Make here and there a gruesome graveless spot
Where someone drank the scorching hotness and is not.
God must have made thee in His anger, and forgot.

ANNE REEVE ALDRICH
1866–1922

Anne Reeve Aldrich was the daughter of the poet James Aldrich, who died when she was eight years old. Her fondness for writing began when she was only a child herself, and she wrote her first verses when she was fifteen. She was first published at seventeen, in *Lippincott's* magazine, and she continued to write for the *Century*, *Scribner's*, and

Lippincott's. Her books include *The Rose of Flame and Other Poems of Love* (1889), *The Feet of Love* (1890), and *Songs about Love, Life and Death*, published posthumously in 1892.

A Little Parable

I made the cross myself whose weight
    Was later laid on me.
This thought is torture as I toil
    Up life's steep Calvary.

To think mine own hands drove the nails!
    I sang a merry song,
And chose the heaviest wood I had
    To build it firm and strong.

If I had guessed – if I had dreamed
    Its weight was meant for me,
I should have made a lighter cross
    To bear up Calvary!

SUSAN MITCHELL
1866–1926

Susan Langstaff Mitchell was born at Carrick-on-Suir, County Leitrim, the daughter of the manager of the local Provincial Bank. He died when she was six, and she was sent to live with two aunts in Dublin. She went to school there, and had lessons in all the standard female accomplishments such as French, drawing and dancing. In 1900 she went to London for treatment for an illness that damaged her hearing and stayed with the Yeats family. The following year she became assistant editor of the *Irish Homestead*, and contributed essays, poems and drama notes to it. Her first collection of verse appeared in 1908, but it is *The Living Chalice and Other Poems*, also published in 1908, for which she is best known.

Love's Mendicant

What do I want of thee?
No gift of smile or tear
Nor casual company,
But in still speech to me
Only thy heart to hear.

Others contentedly
Go lonely here and there;
I cannot pass thee by,
Love's Mendicant am I
Who meet thee everywhere.

No merchandise I make;
Thou mayst not give to me
The counterfeits they take.
I claim Him for Love's sake,
The Hidden One in thee.

The Living Chalice

The Mother sent me on the holy quest,
Timid and proud and curiously dressed
In vestures by her hand wrought wondrously;
An eager burning heart she gave to me.
The Bridegroom's Feast was set and I drew nigh –
Master of Life, Thy Cup has passed me by.

Before new-dressed I from the Mother came,
In dreams I saw the wondrous Cup of Flame.
Ah, Divine Chalice, how my heart drank deep,
Waking I sought the Love I knew asleep.
The Feast of Life was set and I drew nigh –
Master of Life, Thy Cup has passed me by.

Eye of the Soul, awake, awake and see
Growing within the Ruby Radiant Tree,
Sharp pain hath wrung the Clusters of my Vine;
My heart is rose-red with its brimmèd wine.
Thou hast new-set the Feast and I draw nigh –
Master of Life, take me, Thy Cup am I.

CHARLOTTE MEW
1869–1928

Charlotte Mew was born in central London, daughter of Frederick
Mew, an architect, and his wife Anne, daughter of another well-known
architect, Henry Kendall. She spent almost all her life in Bloomsbury,
and lived for thirty years in the same house, number 9 Gordon Street.
Both her younger sister Freda and her younger brother Henry became
mentally ill, with the result that Charlotte and her elder sister Anne
vowed never to marry so as not to pass the disease on.

After their father's death, both sisters began to work. Anne as a
furniture restorer and Charlotte as a writer. She contributed stories to
a variety of magazines and wrote for the *Yellow Book*, the *Nation*, the
New Statesman, the *English Woman* and the *Egoist*. Her most
important poem was 'The Farmer's Bride', published in the *Nation* in
1912. After that she became well-known as a figure on the edge of the
Bloomsbury set.

By 1916, she had virtually stopped writing, and in her last years

produced no prose and only a handful of poems. Her mother died in
1923 and her sister Anne painfully of cancer in 1927. Charlotte never
recovered from those losses and killed herself in a nursing home in
1928.

In Nunhead Cemetery

It is the clay that makes the earth stick to his spade;
    He fills in holes like this year after year;
The others have gone; they were tired, and half afraid,
    But I would rather be standing here;

There is nowhere else to go. I have seen this place
    From the windows of the train that's going past
Against the sky. This is rain on my face –
    It was raining here when I saw it last.

There is something horrible about a flower;
    This, broken in my hand, is one of those
He threw in just now: it will not live another hour;
    There are thousands more: you do not miss a rose.

One of the children hanging about
    Pointed at the whole dreadful heap and smiled
This morning, after *that* was carried out;
    There is something terrible about a child.

We were like children, last week, in the Strand;
    That was the day you laughed at me
Because I tried to make you understand
    The cheap, stale chap I used to be
    Before I saw the things you made me see.

This is not a real place; perhaps by-and-by
　　I shall wake – I am getting drenched with all this rain:
To-morrow I will tell you about the eyes of the Crystal Palace train
　　　Looking down on us, and you will laugh and I shall see what you
　　　see again.

　　　　Not here, not now. We said, 'Not yet
　　　　Across our low stone parapet
　　　Will the quick shadows of the sparrows fall.'
　　　　　But still it was a lovely thing
　　　　　Through the grey months to wait for Spring
　　　　　With the birds that go a-gypsying
　　　In the parks till the blue seas call.
　　　　　And next to these, you used to care
　　　　　For the lions in Trafalgar Square,
Who'll stand and speak for London when her bell of Judgment tolls –
　　　　　And the gulls at Westminster that were
　　　　　The old sea-captains' souls.
To-day again the brown tide splashes, step by step, the river stair,
　　　And the gulls are there!

By a month we have missed our Day:
　　　The children would have hung about
Round the carriage and over the way
　　　As you and I came out.

We should have stood on the gulls' black cliffs and heard the sea
　　　And seen the moon's white track,
I would have called, you would have come to me
　　　And kissed me back.

You have never done that: I do not know
　　　Why I stood staring at your bed
And heard you, though you spoke so low,
　　　But could not reach your hands, your little head.
There was nothing we could not do, you said,
　　　And you went, and I let you go!

Now I will burn you back, I will burn you through,
    Though I am damned for it we two will lie
    And burn, here where the starlings fly
    To these white stones from the wet sky –;
        Dear, you will say this is not I –
It would not be you, it would not be you!

If for only a little while
    You will think of it you will understand,
        If you will touch my sleeve and smile
    As you did that morning in the Strand
        I can wait quietly with you
        Or go away if you want me to –
God! What is God? but your face has gone and your hand!
        Let me stay here too.

        When I was quite a little lad
        At Christmas time we went half mad
        For joy of all the toys we had,
    And then we used to sing about the sheep
        The shepherds watched by night;
    We used to pray to Christ to keep
        Our small souls safe till morning light –;
I am scared, I am staying with you to-night –
        Put me to sleep.

I shall stay here: here you can see the sky;
The houses in the streets are much too high;
        There is no one left to speak to there;
        Here they are everywhere,
And just above them fields and fields of roses lie –
If he would dig it all up again they would not die.

Exspecto Resurrectionem

Oh! King who hast the key
    Of that dark room,
The last which prisons us but held not Thee,
    Thou know'st its gloom.
Dost Thou a little love this one
    Shut in to-night,
Young and so piteously alone,
    Cold – out of sight?
Thou know'st how hard and bare
The pillow of that new-made narrow bed,
    Then leave not there
    So dear a head!

Smile, Death

Smile, Death, see I smile as I come to you
    Straight from the road and the moor that I leave behind,
Nothing on earth to me was like this wind-blown space,
Nothing was like the road, but at the end there was a vision or a face
    And the eyes were not always kind.

    Smile, Death, as you fasten the blades to my feet for me,
On, on let us skate past the sleeping willows dusted with snow;
Fast, fast down the frozen stream, with the moor and the road and the
    vision behind,
    (Show me your face, why the eyes are kind!)
And we will not speak of life or believe in it or remember it as we go.

To a Child in Death

You would have scoffed if we had told you yesterday
   Love made us feel, or so it was with me, like some great bird
      Trying to hold and shelter you in its strong wing –
A gay little shadowy smile would have tossed us back such a solemn
   word,
      And it was not for that you were listening
      When so quietly you slipped away
With half the music of the world unheard.
What shall we do with this strange summer, meant for you –
      Dear, if we see the winter through
      What shall be done with spring?
This, this is the victory of the Grave; here is death's sting,
That it is not strong enough, our strongest wing.

But what of His who like a Father pitieth?
His Son was also, once, a little thing,
The wistfullest child that ever drew breath,
Chased by a sword from Bethlehem and in the busy house at Nazareth
Playing with little rows of nails, watching the carpenter's hammer
   swing,
Long years before His hands and feet were tied
And by a hammer and the three great nails He died,
      Of youth, of Spring,
Of sorrow, of loneliness, of victory the King,
      Under the shadow of that wing.

At the Convent Gate

'Why do you shrink away, and start and stare?
    Life frowns to see you leaning at death's gate –
Not back, but on. Ah! sweet, it is too late:
You cannot cast these kisses from your hair.
Will God's cold breath blow kindly anywhere
    Upon such burning gold? Oh! lips worn white
    With waiting! Love will blossom in a night
And you shall wake to find the roses there!'

'Oh hush! He seems to stir, He lifts His Head.
He smiles. Look where He hangs against the sky.
He never smiled nor stirred, that God of pain
With tired eyes and limbs above my bed –
But loose me, this is death, I will not die –
Not while He smiles. Oh! Christ, Thine own again!'

She was a Sinner

Love was my flower, and before He came –
    'Master, there was a garden where it grew
Rank, with the colour of a crimson flame,
    Thy flower too, but knowing not its name
Nor yet that it was Thine, I did not spare
But tore and trampled it and stained my hair,
My hands, my lips, with the red petals; see,
    Drenched with the blood of Thy poor murdered flower
I stood, when suddenly the hour
        Struck for me,
And straight I came and wound about Thy Feet
        The strands of shame
Twined with those broken buds: till lo, more sweet,
    More red, yet still the same,
Bright burning blossoms sprang around Thy brow
Beneath the thorns (I saw, I know not how,

The crown which Thou wast afterward to wear
   On that immortal Tree)
And I went out and found my garden very bare,
But swept and watered it, then followed Thee.

There was another garden where to seek
Thee, first, I came in those grey hours
Of the Great Dawn, and knew Thee not till Thou didst speak
My name, that 'Mary' like a flash of light
Shot from Thy lips. Thou wast 'the gardener' too,
      And then I knew
That evermore our flowers,
Thine, Lord, and mine, shall be a burning white.'

The Trees are Down

   – and he cried with a loud voice:
   Hurt not the earth, neither the sea, nor the trees –
                   Revelation

They are cutting down the great plane-trees at the end of the gardens.
For days there has been the grate of the saw, the swish of the branches
   as they fall,
The crash of trunks, the rustle of trodden leaves,
With the 'Whoops' and the 'Whoas', the loud common talk, the loud
   common laughs of the men, above it all.

I remember one evening of a long past Spring
Turning in at a gate, getting out of a cart, and finding a large dead rat
   in the mud of the drive.
I remember thinking: alive or dead, a rat was a god-forsaken thing,
But at least, in May, that even a rat should be alive.

The week's work here is as good as done. There is just one bough
  On the roped bole, in the fine grey rain,
        Green and high
        And lonely against the sky.
        (Down now! –)
        And but for that,
        If an old dead rat
Did once, for a moment, unmake the Spring, I might never have
thought of him again.

It is not for a moment the Spring is unmade to-day;
These were great trees, it was in them from root to stem:
When the men with the 'Whoops' and the 'Whoas' have carted the
  whole of the whispering loveliness away
Half the Spring, for me, will have gone with them.

It is going now, and my heart has been struck with the hearts of the
  planes;
Half my life it has beat with these, in the sun, in the rains,
        In the March wind, the May breeze,
In the great gales that came over to them across the roofs from the
  great seas.
        There was only a quiet rain when they were dying;
        They must have heard the sparrows flying,
And the small creeping creatures in the earth where they were lying –
        But I, all day, I heard an angel crying:
        'Hurt not the trees.'

                          Epitaph

            He loved gay things
                Yet with the brave
        He laughed when he was covered with grey wings,
        – Asking the darkest angel for bright things
                And the angel gave –
        So with a smile he overstepped the grave.

EVA GORE-BOOTH
1870–1926

Eva Gore-Booth was born in Lissadell, County Sligo, the daughter of Anglo-Irish landowners. Her sister was the distinguished Irish patriot, and first woman MP, Constance Markievicz, and their childhood was ruled by governesses and by growing socialist thought. Eva went to live in Manchester with her friend Esther Roper, and carried on a career in political and social work for women from 1896 to her death. She produced her first volume of poetry in 1898, and then published both poetry and prose constantly for the rest of her life. Her later writing tends towards the mystical and spiritual, and in the 1990s she is being rediscovered and recognised as an important poet.

The Quest

For years I sought the Many in the One,
I thought to find lost waves and broken rays,
The rainbow's faded colours in the sun –
The dawns and twilights of forgotten days.

But now I seek the One in every form,
Scorning no vision that a dewdrop holds,
The gentle Light that shines behind the storm,
The Dream that many a twilight hour enfolds.

Harvest

Though the long seasons seem to separate
Sower and reaper or deeds dreamed and done,
Yet when a man reaches the Ivory Gate
Labour and life and seed and corn are one.

Because thou art the doer and the deed,
Because thou art the thinker and the thought,
Because thou art the helper and the need,
And the cold doubt that brings all things to nought.

Therefore in every gracious form and shape
The world's dear open secret shalt thou find,
From the One Beauty there is no escape
Nor from the sunshine of the Eternal mind.

The patient labourer, with guesses dim,
Follows this wisdom to its secret goal.
He knows all deeds and dreams exist in him,
And all men's God in every human soul.

Form

The buried statue through the marble gleams,
Praying for freedom, an unwilling guest,
Yet flooding with the light of her strange dreams
The hard stone folded round her uncarved breast.

Founded in granite, wrapped in serpentine,
Light of all life and heart of every storm,
Doth the uncarven image, the Divine,
Deep in the heart of each man, wait for form.

BEATRICE RAVENEL
1870–1956

Beatrice Ravenel was educated privately and enrolled at the women's section of Harvard in 1889. There she played an important role amongst a group of literary young people including Vaughn Moody and Trumbull Stickney. She wrote for the *Harvard Monthly*, the *Advocate*, *Scribner's* and the *Literary Digest*.

In 1900 she married Francis Gualdo Ravenel whose mother was a famous writer, Harriet Horry Ravenel. They lived on a plantation south of Charleston, and Beatrice wrote. But her husband went through her money, and she ended up supporting the family with her writing for *Ainslie's*, *Harper's*, and the *Saturday Evening Post*.

She started writing poetry again in 1910, and in the 1920s underwent a complete change of style, producing vivid free verse of great accomplishment. She met other poets through the newly formed South Carolina Poetry Society, and made friends with Amy Lowell when she came to visit. Her first husband died in 1920 and she married his relative Samuel Prioleau Ravenel in 1926. She no longer needed to write for financial reward, but some of her best poetry, especially that set in the West Indies, dates from this later period.

The Day You Went

The day you went my world was done.
There came no comfort from the sun
Nor from the love of life that lurks
In sunlight, nor from all the works
Of faith and old philosophy –
Till one young rose leaned down to me
And shot my brooding like a wing –
The most foolhardy, gallant thing
In all this rocking world, conceived
Of morning dew . . . and I believed
It bannered upward from the sod
The visible defense of God.

LEONORA SPEYER
1872–1956

Leonora Speyer was the daughter of a Prussian officer who fought for
the Union in the American Civil War and of a New England mother.
Her first career was as a violinist: she made her debut at eighteen with
the Boston Symphony, and then went to the New York Philharmonic.
She had four daughters by her first husband, but the marriage ended in
divorce, and she married Sir Edward Speyer, a banker, in 1902. In 1915
the couple moved permanently to the USA, and when he was smitten
with acute neuritis, Leonora, no longer able to play the violin, took to
writing poetry seriously. She was regarded very highly, winning the
Pulitzer Prize in 1927 for her second volume of poems, and becoming
President of the Poetry Society of America in 1934.

   She was influenced by Amy Lowell, a close friend, and by Edna St
Vincent Millay. Her poetry can be sentimental and even precious, but
on the whole she achieved an almost melodious flow, and her many
nature poems are probably her finest work.

Duet

I Sing with Myself

Out of my sorrow
I'll build a stair,
And every to-morrow
Will climb to me there –

*With ashes of yesterday
In its hair.*

My fortune is made
Of a stab in the side,
My debts are paid
In pennies of pride –

Unminted coins
In a heart I hide.

The stones that I eat
Are ripe for my needs,
My cup is complete
With the dregs of deeds –

Clear are the notes
Of my broken reeds.

I carry my pack
Of aches and stings,
Light with the lack
Of all good things –

But not on my back,
Because of my wings!

Let Not My Death Be Long

Let not my death be long,
But light
As a bird's swinging;
Happy decision in the height
Of song –
Then flight
From off the ultimate bough!
And let my wing be strong,
And my last note the first
Of another's singing.
See to it, Thou.

Protest in Passing

This house of flesh was never loved of me,
Though I have known much love beneath its roof,
Always was I a guest who stood aloof,
Loth to accept such hospitality.
When the house slumbered, how I woke! for then
I knew of half-escapes along the night,
But now there comes a safer, swifter flight:
I go; nor need endure these rooms again.

I have been cowed too long by closed-in walls,
By masonry of muscle, blood and bone;
This quaking house of flesh that was my own,
High roof-tree of the heart, see how it falls!
I go . . . but pause upon the threshold's rust
To shake from off my feet my own dead dust.

LOLA RIDGE
1873–1941

Lola Ridge came originally from Dublin, but travelled with her mother
via Australia and New Zealand to New York. She married the manager
of a New Zealand gold mine, but when that marriage failed, she went
to Sydney to study painting. She emigrated to San Francisco in 1907,
and moved to New York in 1908, where she spent much of the rest of
her life.

In 1918 she published *The Ghetto*, a collection of long poems
dwelling on courage amongst ordinary people, in this case the Jews of
the Lower East Side. She also edited and lectured, and married again in
1919.

Her poetry was both personal and political. 'The Red Flag' (1927)
focuses on the Russian Revolution. and many of her poems touch on

social issues of her day, with a clearly liberal and left-wing stance. Her later years were filled with more mystical endeavours, including an attempt, which she did not live to complete, to write a major poetry cycle running through from ancient Babylon to Manhattan after the First World War.

Sons of Belial

We are old,
Old as song.
Before Rome was
Or Cyrene.
Mad nights knew us
And old men's wives.
We knew who spilled the sacred oil
For young-gold harlots of the town....
We knew where the peacocks went
And the white doe for sacrifice.

We were the sons of Belial.
One black night
Centuries ago
We beat at a door
In Gilead....
We took the Levite's concubine
We plucked her hands from off the door....
We choked the cry into her throat
And stuck the stars among her hair....
We glimpsed the madly swaying stars
Between the rhythms of her hair....
And all our mute and separate strings
Swelled in a raging symphony....
All that night our blood sang pæans
Till dawn fell like a wounded swan
Upon the fields of Gilead.

We are old. . . .
Old as song. . . .
    We are dumb song.
(*Epics tingled*
In our blood
When we haled Hypatia
Over the stones
In Alexandria.)
Could we loose
The wild rhythms clinched in us. . . .
March in bands of troubadours. . . .
We would be of gentle mood.
When Christ healed us
Who were dumb –
When he freed our shut-in song –
We strewed green palms
At his pale feet. . . .
We sang hosannas
In Jerusalem.
And all our fumbling voices blent
In a brief white harmony.
(*But a mightier song*
Was in us pent
When we nailed Christ
To a four-armed tree.)

We are young.
When we rise up with singing roots,
(*Warm rains washing*
Gutters of Berlin
Where we stamped Rosa . . . Luxemburg
On a night in spring.)
Rhythms skurry in our blood.
Little nimble rats of song
In our feet run crazily
And all is dust . . . we trample . . . on.
Mad nights when we make ritual

(Feet running before the sleuth-light ...
And the smell of burnt flesh
By a flame-ringed hut
In Missouri,
Sweet as on Rome's pyre. ...)
We make ropes do rigadoons
With copper feet that jig on air. . . .
We are the Mob. . . .
Old as song. . . .
Tyre knew us
And Israel.

The Ghetto

Lights go out
And the stark trunks of the factories
Melt into the drawn darkness,
Sheathing like a seamless garment.
And mothers take home their babies,
Waxen and delicately curled,
Like little potted flowers closed under the stars. . . .

Lights go out . . .
And colors rush together,
Fusing and floating away.
Pale worn gold like the settings of old jewels . . .
Mauve, exquisite, tremulous, and luminous purples,
And burning spires in aureoles of light
Like shimmering auras.

They are covering up the pushcarts . . .
Now all have gone save an old man with mirrors –
Little oval mirrors like tiny pools.
He shuffles up a darkened street

And the moon burnishes his mirrors till they shine like phosphorus. . . .
The moon like a skull,
Staring out of eyeless sockets at the old men trundling home the
pushcarts.

AMY LOWELL
1874–1925

Amy Lowell came from a family of well-known New England
intellectuals, part of the Boston brahmin society. She disapproved of
wasting time or money, on the grounds that she was 'an old-fashioned
Puritan', but her lifestyle, though unfrivolous, was certainly expensive.

She was a real campaigner for poetry, and she became prominent in
literary circles, particularly after 1913 amongst the Imagists. She took
on the task of re-educating the American taste, and her campaigning
for poetry brought her a mixture of acclaim and attacks.

There are a few great poems amongst her work, but her poetry,
although it was the basis of her career, is not what makes her
memorable. Rather, it was her campaigning, her forcefulness, her
impresario-like qualities, that made her great, and her feeling that real
poetry could be learned and encouraged in what she saw as an
uncivilised setting.

Patterns

I walk down the garden paths,
And all the daffodils
Are blowing, and the bright blue squills.
I walk down the patterned garden-paths
In my stiff, brocaded gown.
With my powdered hair and jewelled fan.

I too am a rare
Pattern. As I wander down
The garden paths.

My dress is richly figured,
    And the train
Makes a pink and silver stain
On the gravel, and the thrift
Of the borders.
Just a plate of current fashion,
Tripping by in high-heeled, ribboned shoes.

Not a softness anywhere about me,
Only whalebone and brocade.
And I sink on a seat in the shade
Of a lime tree. For my passion
Wars against the stiff brocade.
The daffodils and squills
Flutter in the breeze
As they please.
And I weep;
For the lime tree is in blossom
And one small flower has dropped upon my bosom.

And the plashing of waterdrops
In the marble fountain
Comes down the garden-paths.
The dripping never stops.
Underneath my stiffened gown
Is the softness of a woman bathing in a marble basin,
A basin in the midst of hedges grown
So thick, she cannot see her lover hiding,
But she guesses he is near,
And the sliding of the water
Seems the stroking of a dear
Hand upon her.

What is Summer in a fine brocaded gown!
I should like to see it lying in a heap upon the ground.
All the pink and silver crumpled up on the ground.
I would be the pink and silver as I ran along the paths,
And he would stumble after,
Bewildered by my laughter.
I should see the sun flashing from his sword-hilt and the buckles on his
    shoes.
I would choose
To lead him in a maze along the patterned paths,
A bright and laughing maze for my heavy-booted lover.

Till he caught me in the shade,
And the buttons of his waistcoat bruised my body as he clasped me,
Aching, melting, unafraid.
With the shadows of the leaves and the sundrops,
And the plopping of the waterdrops,
All about us in the open afternoon –
I am very like to swoon
With the weight of this brocade,
For the sun sifts through the shade.

Underneath the fallen blossom
In my bosom,
Is a letter I have hid.
It was brought to me this morning by a rider from the Duke.
'Madam, we regret to inform you that Lord Hartwell
Died in action Thursday se'nnight.'
As I read it in the white, morning sunlight,
The letters squirmed like snakes.
'Any answer, Madam,' said my footman.
'No,' I told him.
'See that the messenger takes some refreshment.
No, no answer.'
And I walked into the garden,
Up and down the patterned paths,
In my stiff, correct brocade.

The blue and yellow flowers stood up proudly in the sun,
Each one.
I stood upright too,
Held rigid to the pattern
By the stiffness of my gown.
Up and down I walked,
Up and down.

In a month he would have been my husband.
In a month, here, underneath this lime,
We would have broke the pattern;
He for me, and I for him,
He as Colonel, I as Lady,
On this shady seat.
He had a whim
That sunlight carried blessing.
And I answered, 'It shall be as you have said.'
Now he is dead.

In Summer and in Winter I shall walk
Up and down
The patterned garden-paths
In my stiff, brocaded gown.
The squills and daffodils
Will give place to pillared roses, and to asters, and to snow.
I shall go
Up and down
In my gown.
Gorgeously arrayed,
Boned and stayed.
And the softness of my body will be guarded from embrace
By each button, hook, and lace.
For the man who should loose me is dead,
Fighting with the Duke in Flanders,
In a pattern called a war.
Christ! What are patterns for?

THEODOSIA GARRISON
1874–1944

Theodosia Garrison was born in Newark, New Jersey, and was the author of several volumes of poetry very popular in their day. These included *Joy o' Life and Other Poems* (1909), *Earth Cry and Other Poems* (1910), *The Dreamers and Other Poems* (1912) and *As the Larks Rise* (1921). She married Frederic Faulks, but continued to use her own name for her writing.

Stains

The three ghosts on the lonesome road
  Spake each to one another,
'Whence came that stain about your mouth
  No lifted hand may cover?'
'From eating of forbidden fruit,
  Brother, my brother.'

The three ghosts on the sunless road
  Spake each to one another,
'Whence came that red burn on your foot
  No dust nor ash may cover?'
'I stamped a neighbor's hearth-flame out,
  Brother, my brother.'

The three ghosts on the windless road
  Spake each to one another,
'Whence came that blood upon your hand
  No other hand may cover?'
'From breaking of a woman's heart,
  Brother, my brother.'

'Yet on the earth clean men we walked,
Glutton and Thief and Lover;
White flesh and fair it hid our stains
That no man might discover.'
'Naked the soul goes up to God,
Brother, my brother.'

ADELAIDE CRAPSEY
1878–1914

Adelaide Crapsey became a legendary figure within a year of her death, when a slender volume of her poems, entitled *Verse*, appeared. It contained the brief writings of her short life, and in them she depicted her isolation and her relationship with death, as a prisoner, as it were. She had spent a year in Rome from 1905–1906 and at some stage of her travels abroad she contracted tuberculosis. After a total physical breakdown, she went to Saranac Lake to recuperate; her windows there overlooked the graveyard called Trudeau's Garden, about which she wrote.

Her year of supposed convalescence did her no good and she died in 1914, having contributed an original verse form, the cinquain, not entirely dissimilar to the Japanese haiku, to the English language.

The Warning

Just now,
Out of the strange
Still dusk . . . as strange, as still . . .
A white moth flew. Why am I grown
So cold?

Triad

These be
Three silent things:
The falling snow ... the hour
Before the dawn ... the mouth of one
Just dead.

The Lonely Death

In the cold I will rise, I will bathe
In waters of ice; myself
Will shiver, and shrive myself,
Alone in the dawn, and anoint
Forehead and feet and hands;
I will shutter the windows from light,
I will place in their sockets the four
Tall candles and set them aflame
In the grey of the dawn; and myself
Will lay myself straight in my bed,
And draw the sheet under my chin.

JOSEPHINE ROYLE

Josephine Royle was American, her work is published in Edwin Markham's excellent anthology, *The Book of American Poetry*, and she was presumably still alive when it was reprinted in 1934. Beyond that, I can find out nothing about her and can only guess at where she should appear in this chronological survey. Nevertheless, her verse is so appealing that these two short examples deserve their place here.

Deep Peace

I belong to the tide,
I belong to the sea,
All of its changing and restless life,
All of its ceaseless and endless strife,
These are a part of me;
But there is a peace in the depths of the sea,
Like the peace that is deep in the heart of me.

Give Us This Day

Today I pray for one thing,
Tomorrow quite another,
I am afraid that I give God
An awful lot of bother.

EDITH SITWELL
1887–1964

Despite professing to loathe women's poetry (with the notable exception of Christina Rossetti), Edith Sitwell wrote verse from the age of seventeen and published volumes of it from 1915 onwards. She set up the annual *Wheels* with her brothers Osbert and Sacheverell, and wrote for it much that was anti-war.

Her later works included biographies of Elizabeth I, Queen Victoria and Pope, and a biographical novel about Swift, *I Live Under a Black Sun*. She was made a DBE in 1954. Having been intrigued by Roman Catholicism for many years, she finally converted in 1955.

Still Falls the Rain

The Raids, 1940. Night and Dawn

Still falls the Rain –
Dark as the world of man, black as our loss –
Blind as the nineteen hundred and forty nails
Upon the Cross.

Still falls the Rain
With a sound like the pulse of the heart that is changed to the hammer-
    beat
In the Potter's Field, and the sound of the impious feet

On the Tomb:
                    Still falls the Rain
In the Field of Blood where the small hopes breed and the human brain
Nurtures its greed, that worm with the brow of Cain.

Still falls the Rain
At the feet of the Starved Man hung upon the Cross.
Christ that each day, each night, nails there,
                        have mercy on us –
On Dives and on Lazarus:
Under the Rain the sore and the gold are as one.

Still falls the Rain –
Still falls the Blood from the Starved Man's wounded Side:
He bears in his Heart all wounds, – those of the light
                        that died,
The last faint spark
In the self-murdered heart, the wounds of the sad
                        uncomprehending dark,
The wounds of the baited bear, –
The blind and weeping bear whom the keepers beat
On his helpless flesh . . . the tears of the hunted hare.

Still falls the Rain –
Then – O Ile leape up to my God: who pulles me doune –
See, see where Christ's blood streames in the firmament:
It flows from the Brow we nailed upon the tree
Deep to the dying, to the thirsting heart
That holds the fires of the world, – dark-smirched with pain
As Caesar's laurel crown.

Then sounds the voice of One who like the heart of man
Was once a child who among beasts has lain –
'Still do I love, still shed my innocent light, my Blood, for thee.'

ELINOR WYLIE
1885–1928

Elinor Wylie was born into a politically prominent family in Philadelphia and Washington, and her abandonment of her first husband and son to elope with a married Washington lawyer, Horace Wylie, became a *cause célèbre*. The couple lived in England as Mr and Mrs Horace Waring and it was there that Elinor published her first book of poetry, anonymously, under the title *Incidental Numbers*.

The Wylies returned to the USA before the outbreak of the First World War and lived in Boston, then Augusta, Georgia, and lastly back in Washington, seat of the scandal they had caused. Elinor became friendly with the prominent writers of the time, including Edmund Wilson, John Dos Passos and William Rose Benet, and she divorced Wylie for Benet in 1923.

She died aged only forty-three, but by that time had produced a large body of poetry, as well as serving as contributing editor to the *New Republic* for several years. Her poetry is mixed in style and subject matter, but she expresses well the tensions of her calm, beautiful exterior and the turbulent passions within her soul. Many critics abhor

her work, but in her best poems she has an original voice and a very
personal, sometimes agonised, message.

Hymn to Earth

Farewell, incomparable element,
Whence man arose, where he shall not return;
And hail, imperfect urn
Of his last ashes, and his firstborn fruit;
Farewell, the long pursuit,
And all the adventures of his discontent;
The voyages which sent
His heart averse from home:
Metal of clay, permit him that he come
To thy slow-burning fire as to a hearth;
Accept him as a particle of earth.

Fire, being divided from the other three,
It lives removed, or secret at the core;
Most subtle of the four,
When air flies not, nor water flows,
It disembodied goes,
Being light, elixir of the first decree,
More volatile than he;
With strength and power to pass
Through space, where never his least atom was:
He has no part in it, save as his eyes
Have drawn its emanation from the skies.

A wingless creature heavier than air,
He is rejected of its quintessence;
Coming and going hence,
In the twin minutes of his birth and death,
He may inhale as breath,
As breath relinquish heaven's atmosphere,
Yet in it have no share,

Nor can survive therein
Where its outer edge is filtered pure and thin:
It doth but lend its crystal to his lungs
For his early crying, and his final songs.

The element of water has denied
Its child; it is no more his element;
It never will relent;
Its silver harvests are more sparsely given
Than the rewards of heaven,
And he shall drink cold comfort at its side:
The water is too wide:
The seamew and the gull
Feather a nest made soft and pitiful
Upon its foam; he has not any part
In the long swell of sorrow at its heart.

Hail and farewell, belovèd element,
Whence he departed, and his parent once;
See where thy spirit runs
Which for so long hath had the moon to wife;
Shall this support his life
Until the arches of the waves be bent
And grow shallow and spent?
Wisely it cast him forth
With his dead weight of burdens nothing worth,
Leaving him, for the universal years,
A little sea water to make his tears.

Hail, element of earth, receive thy own,
And cherish, at thy charitable breast,
This man, this mongrel beast:
He ploughs the sand, and, at his hardest need,
He sows himself for seed;
He ploughs the furrow, and in this lies down
Before the corn is grown;
Between the apple bloom

And the ripe apple is sufficient room
In time, and matter, to consume his love
And make him parcel of a cypress grove.

Receive him as thy lover for an hour
Who will not weary, by a longer stay,
The kind embrace of clay;
Even within thine arms he is dispersed
To nothing, as at first;
The air flings downward from its four-quartered tower
Him whom the flames devour;
At the full tide, at the flood,
The sea is mingled with his salty blood:
The traveller dust, although the dust be vile,
Sleeps as thy lover for a little while.

Prophecy

I shall lie hidden in a hut
    In the middle of an alder wood,
With the back door blind and bolted shut,
    And the front door locked for good.

I shall lie folded like a saint,
    Lapped in a scented linen sheet,
On a bedstead striped with bright-blue paint,
    Narrow and cold and neat.

The midnight will be glassy black
    Behind the panes, with wind about
To set his mouth against a crack
    And blow the candle out.

FRANCES CORNFORD
1886–1960

Frances Cornford was born a Darwin, one of the famous scientific family. Her mother died when she was seventeen. Her social circle was therefore that of the wider family, as described by Gwen Raverat, her cousin, in *Period Piece*, a charming account of the Darwin set as it existed in and around Cambridge and the particular quality of their intellectually free lives. Frances married the classical scholar Francis Cornford in 1908, and they had a poet son, John, who was killed in the Spanish Civil War in 1936.

Between 1910 and 1960 Frances published eight volumes of poetry, winning the Queen's Medal for Poetry in 1959. She also translated poetry from Russian in collaboration with Esther Salamon, and from French with Stephen Spender. Her poetry has been much underrated, both by G. K. Chesterton, who was scathing in his criticism, and by later assessors, including John Galassi, who edited a volume of the writings of John Cornford. In fact, she writes lyrically of the beauty of Cambridge, and with real pain about war, about the difference between the sexes, and about female isolation. Her best known lines are on this last theme: 'O fat white woman whom nobody loves, Why do you walk through the field in gloves?'

Frances Cornford is being re-evaluated by a series of modern critics, and is clearly destined to be considered a far more significant poet than has previously been recognised.

The Trumpet Shall Sound

MESSIAH 1742

We who are met to celebrate
Grandly today our God and King and State
   'We shall be changed' – but shall not change too far:
Twice as superb will be, and twice as big
   Each fair, abounding, and immortal wig;
   And every button on our coats, a star.

Where Lords and Commons ever equal are
Each regal coach will grow a wingèd car,
Whose laurelled lackeys in triumphant light
Sing their symmetrical delight;
And link-boys with the flaming cherubim
Dance in their buckled shoes and shout the morning hymn;
Where coachmen crowned with asphodel and moly
Echo the cries of Holy, Holy, Holy;
And disembodied horses fly
With golden trumpeters about the sky.

O we shall change, but with no pangs of birth,
To glorious heaven from this glorious earth.

The Revelation

In my dark mind you kicked a stone away.
There in the light, a full-grown Purpose lay;
And half in terror, half in glad surprise
I saw his unknown coils and sleeping eyes.

H.D. (HILDA DOOLITTLE)
1886–1961

Hilda Doolittle was born in Bethlehem, Pennsylvania, into a family of
Moravian Protestants. As a student she was briefly engaged to Ezra
Pound, and travelled to London to see him in 1911.

In London, Pound introduced her to the entire literary scene. She
met Flint, Hulme and Aldington, who formed the short-lived Imagist
movement, and married Richard Aldington in 1913. At that point she
started to publish some of her poems, and they enjoyed considerable

success from 1916 onwards. But her personal life was a mess and a series of tragedies led to a near breakdown, which she described as 'psychic death'. The disasters included the deaths of her father and older brother, a miscarriage and her separation from Aldington.

But recovery came with her relationship with Winifred Ellerman, a novelist who came to see her after admiring her poems. They became lovers and travelled to Greece, America and Egypt with H.D.'s newborn daughter Perdita in tow. Her experience of lesbianism and the visits to Greece made H.D. more and more fascinated by the Greek world, and in 1924 she published *Heliodora and Other Poems*, in which gods and goddesses are in conversation. A play, *Hippolytus Temporised*, followed in 1927.

In the 1930s H.D. was analysed by Freud, an experience which made her increasingly fascinated with her own sexuality and with the role of women. Her later writings are more consciously feminist, and the verse drama *Helen in Egypt*, probably her last work, was published in 1961, telling the story of the Trojan War from a feminist and feminine perspective. Her work is now being constantly reassessed, and her reputation is rising as a serious literary star of much of this century.

Wine Bowl

I will rise
from my troth
with the dead,
I will sweeten my cup
and my bread
with a gift;
I will chisel a bowl for the wine,
for the white wine
and red;
I will summon a Satyr to dance,
a Centaur,
a Nymph
and a Faun;
I will picture

a warrior King,
a Giant,
a Naiad,
a Monster;
I will cut round the rim of the
    crater,
some simple
familiar thing,
vine leaves
or the sea-swallow's wing;
I will work at each separate part
till my mind is worn out
and my heart:
in my skull,

where the vision had birth,
will come wine,
would pour song
of the hot earth,
of the flower and the sweet
of the hill,
thyme,
meadow-plant,
grass-blade and sorrel;
in my skull,
from which vision took flight,
will come wine
will pour song
of the cool night,
of the silver and blade of the
    moon,
of the star,
of the sun's kiss at mid-noon;
I will challenge the reed-pipe
and stringed lyre,
to sing sweeter,
pipe wilder,
praise louder
the fragrance and sweet
of the wine-jar,
till each lover
must summon another,
to proffer a rose
where all flowers are,
in the depths of the exquisite
    crater;
flower will fall upon flower
till the red shower
inflame all
with intimate fervour;

till:
men who travel afar
will look up,
sensing grape
and hill-slope
in the cup;
men who sleep by the wood
will arise,
hearing ripple and fall
of the tide,
being drawn by the spell of the
    sea;
the bowl will ensnare and enchant
men who crouch by the hearth
till they want
but the riot of stars in the night;
those who dwell far inland
will seek ships;
the deep-sea fisher,
plying his nets,
will forsake them
for wheat-sheaves and loam;
men who wander
will yearn for their home,
men at home
will depart.

*I will rise
from my troth with the dead,
I will sweeten my cup
and my bread
with a gift;
I will chisel a bowl for the wine,
for the white wine
and red.*

DOROTHY WELLESLEY
1889–1956

Dorothy Wellesley was born in Berkshire of Cheshire stock. After her father's death her mother married the tenth Earl of Scarborough. In 1914, Dorothy married Lord Gerald Wellesley, and they had two children. On the death of his father in 1943, Gerald became the Duke and Dorothy the Duchess of Wellington.

She started writing poetry at an astonishingly early age, and was a natural rebel, whose lack of education outside the home made her careless about punctuation and short of intellectual stimulus.

For all that, she was a poet of some considerable art. She proclaimed herself at various times an agnostic, a fiery atheist, a campaigner, a lover of beauty, and she wrote romantically, quickly and inaccurately. Nevertheless, her quirky mind and her endless curiosity and love of nature make some of her poetry well worth reading, and she is enjoying a deserved rediscovery at the end of the century.

The Buried Child

He is not dead nor liveth
The little child in the grave,
And men have known for ever
That he walketh again;
They hear him November evenings,
When acorns fall with the rain.

Deep in the hearts of men
Within his tomb he lieth,
And when the heart is desolate
He desolate sigheth.

Teach me then the heart of the dead child,
Who, holding a tulip, goeth
Up the stairs in his little grave-shift,
Sitting down in his little chair
By his biscuit and orange,
In the nursery he knoweth.

Teach me all that the child who knew life
And the quiet of death,
To the croon of the cradle-song
By his brother's crib
In the deeps of the nursery dusk
To his mother saith.

ANGELA MORGAN
d. 1957

Angela Morgan was born in Washington DC, at an unknown date. She
wrote prolifically, publishing volumes of poetry from 1914 onwards.
These included *The Hour has Struck* (1914), *Because of Beauty* (1922),
Creator Man (1929) and *Gold on Your Pillow*.

Gandhi

Not with a clamor of golden deeds,
Nor girt with brazen armor, doth he come.
No herald trumpets him, on royal steeds,
His armies follow not with martial drum.

*

Have you at times been swept beyond all creed
By some new-dawning Vision of the right,
Your mind ablaze with thoughts of human need,
Drawn heavenward within a wakeful night?
Have you then said, your faint soul strong at last:
'Whatever be the torture of this goal,
Here and here only shall my lot be cast –
This is the plan God fashioned for my soul!'

Then look on Gandhi, Hindu saint and seer;
Lo, in the living flesh behold your vow –
The ancient Truth grown intimate and near,
That God may find His image, here and now.
Here is the heart that dares defy the strain
And terror of conditions as they are:
Here is the sturdy will immune to pain,
Here is the soul that dares become a star!

Here is the noble intellect that saw
Beyond the spasm of our human lust
The silent grandeur of Eternal Law
Wheeling its wingèd way above our dust,
And linked his being with that lofty scheme,
And ordered all his ways, that he might find
Out of the Infinite a way supreme
To bring immortal justice for his kind.

How like a sun he shines above our dearth!
How like a man he leans unto the earth.
He is the answer to your faith and mine –
Man by his love for man, becomes divine.

KATHERINE GARRISON CHAPIN
1890–1977

Katherine Garrison Chapin was a poet, translator and reviewer. She was educated at Columbia University and went straight on to review for the leading journals of her day. She wrote essentially American poetry, leaving the subject of the Second World War largely untouched. But she had one attempt at a metaphysical poem of considerable length, 'The Other Journey', as well as writing a few shorter, less well-known poems on similar themes. Her search for meaning and her calmness of approach make her very different from many of her contemporaries, but she is worth reading for her lack of self-pity and for her extraordinary dignity and spareness of style.

The Other Journey

Valley of ancient life, how many visions died,
In this bright sand, how many dreams were born,
The falcon and the angel side by side,
The limbs of love from bleeding body torn.
Who shall discern the fire on the hill
Or rise again obedient to a will?

Summon the princely chariot from the halls,
The hunter and the hunted, in their chase,
Bright spear suspended. For the one who falls,
Another rises who shall take his place,
And on the timeless surface of the walls,
With deeper line mark out a different face.

The broken fragments of Man's searching lie
In cycles from first dark to later dark;
A goddess sucks the udders of the sky,
Goat-headed Fate sits in his moving barque;
Sirius erect, celestial majesty,
Steers his slight boat across a star-divided sea.

Valley of ancient time, here fresh creation
Lies like a dew upon each living shape
Throbs in singing bird throat, in the motion
Of dancing feet, moves in coil of snake.
The Queen's white garment flutters
As she receives the key of life within her long thin fingers.

And life is center of the Temple's plan
Which moves forever forward in design;
In measure of the microcosm, man,
Man living, not destroyed, not sacrificed
(A drooped Head on a Cross)
But man, source of fertile power, linked with the planet's source.

Where tall papyrus-budded columns rise
In flowering rows, their peristyle and place
Stand in conjunction with revolving skies,
Earth-season rhythms, axis-turn and base;
Man's heart-beat and its blood;
Its time of ebbing and its mounting flood.

Among these living symbols in charged air
Of December desert, through still night and day,
I look beyond the clear horizon for another star,
Search on the hills for that thin ray
Which severed earth and sky, gather
The ancient legends of a Son and Mother.

Isis or Mary, with her Child asleep,
Dipped in the river to wash His swaddling clothes,
And from the drops which fell and settled deep
In Earth, seed sprang, and a dark tree arose,
A bitter balsam tree. Its wide
Branches cut to make the cross on which He died.

O Poet risen from the tomb! The god,
Dead, lives in his son. Death
Of the Son dying that man may find
Again a living breath.
He shall take power from the dead
Nor ask for bleeding testament, nor thorn-crowned head.

Nor ask for pity. Earth is taken by the strong,
The strong in secret wisdom,
Who know the wrath, the violence that belong
To life, from stir of womb and the first cry,
To the last measure of its ecstasy.

EDNA ST VINCENT MILLAY
1892–1950

Edna St Vincent Millay's work is probably the best known of all American poetry of the twentieth century. It is memorable, clever, moving and very carefully written. But it was more popular in her lifetime, as an expression of the hopes of young and emancipated women, than it is now.

Educated at Vassor, she went to live in Greenwich Village, where her mother and sisters joined her. There she was a great social success, being both pretty and charming. The critic Edmund Wilson proposed to her, but she chose to marry Eugen Jan Boissevain, a Dutchman twelve years her senior, who had previously been married to the feminist campaigner Inez Milholland, and who wanted to 'free' Vincent to concentrate on her work and nothing else.

They lived at Steepletop in the southern Berkshires, where they were extremely happy. Vincent travelled a great deal and her poetry was hugely popular. She also wrote opera libretti and became involved in various social crusades, and her later work was increasingly concerned with social and political issues; perhaps as a result she had to watch her popularity wane during the 1930s. Boissevain died in 1949 and she followed him only a year later, dying alone, of a heart attack, with her popularity at its lowest.

However, her early works, especially her sonnets, are creeping back into fashion. Her spiritual interests, in that close, careful form, are masterpieces of the genre.

The Anguish

I would to God I were quenched and fed
As in my youth
From the flask of song, and the good bread
Of beauty richer than truth.

The anguish of the world is on my tongue.
My bowl is filled to the brim with it; there is more than I can eat.
Happy are the toothless old and the toothless young,
That cannot rend this meat.

'What's this of death, from you who will never die?'

What's this of death, from you who never will die?
Think you the wrist that fashioned you in clay,
The thumb that set the hollow just that way
In your full throat and lidded the long eye
So roundly from the forehead, will let lie
Broken, forgotten, under foot some day
Your unimpeachable body, and so slay
The work he most had been remembered by?
I tell you this: whatever of dust to dust
Goes down, whatever of ashes may return
To its essential self in its own season,
Loveliness such as yours will not be lost,
But, cast in bronze upon his very urn,
Make known him Master, and for what good reason.

'I see so clearly now my similar years'

I see so clearly now my similar years
Repeat each other, shod in rusty black,
Like one hack following another hack
In meaningless procession, dry of tears,
Driven empty, lest the noses sharp as shears
Of gutter-urchins at a hearse's back
Should sniff a man died friendless, and attack
With silly scorn his deaf triumphant ears;
I see so clearly how my life must run
One year behind another year until
At length these bones that leap into the sun
Are lowered into the gravel, and lie still,
I would at times the funeral were done
And I abandoned on the ultimate hill.

God's World

O world, I cannot hold thee close enough!
Thy winds, thy wide grey skies!
  Thy mists that roll and rise!
Thy woods this autumn day, that ache and sag
And all but cry with color! That gaunt crag
To crush! To lift the lean of that black bluff!
World, World, I cannot get thee close enough!

Long have I known a glory in it all,
  But never knew I this;
  Here such a passion is
As stretcheth me apart – Lord, I do fear
Thou'st made the world too beautiful this year;
My soul is all but out of me – let fall
No burning leaf; prithee, let no bird call.

Siege

This I do, being mad:
Gather baubles about me,
Sit in a circle of toys, and all the time
Death beating the door in.

White jade and an orange pitcher,
Hindu idol, Chinese god –
Maybe next year, when I'm richer –
Carved beads and a lotus pod....

And all this time
Death beating the door in.

V. SACKVILLE-WEST
1892–1962

Victoria Mary Sackville-West was the daughter of Victoria, illegitimate daughter of the Spanish dancer Pepita and Lionel Sackville-West, and the third Baron Sackville. She was educated at Miss Woolff's school in London, and by governesses at Knole in Kent, the house she loved. She much resented being unable to inherit it by the 'technical fault' of her sex. She wrote *The Heir* in 1922 as a farewell to Knole.

In 1913 she married Harold Nicolson, and they had two sons. Their bisexuality is well known, and their letters and an account of his parents' marriage are edited and written by their son Nigel. Vita's greatest affair was with her childhood friend Violet Keppel (Trefusis), with whom she ran away to Paris in the 1920s.

Vita wrote prolifically – *The Edwardians, Knole and the Sackvilles, Seducers in Ecuador* and *All Passion Spent* being a few of the forty or so volumes she produced. She was close to Virginia Woolf and they

paid each other compliments in their writing, both in Woolf's *Orlando*
and in *All Passion Spent*.

She and Harold bought Sissinghurst Castle, also in Kent, and began
a lifetime of restoration and gardening. The garden is still a major
attraction, in the hands of the National Trust, and her books are being
reissued by a variety of publishers. Her poem 'The Land' won the
Hawthornden Prize, and her writing is increasingly being reread,
though on the whole her poetry is still sadly neglected.

A Dream

Down the long path beneath the garden wall,
She stooped, setting her plants in the winter dusk.
She knew she must make an end of setting her plants,
Though why she must make an end she nothing knew.
Was it the end of the year that made her urgent?
Was it the end of the day? for night came down,
And the heavy sky grew black above the wall,
And the trees were quiet in a stillness worse than storm
As the great white stealthy flakes began to fall,
But still she stooped with her trowel, setting her plants.

And the ground grew white with the imperceptible drift
Of the silent snow from a black and loaded heaven,
And candles came around her, stuck in silver;
Candelabra of silver, with horns of flame,
Burning the snow to a ruddy glow as she set
The fragile year's-end plants of her dying hopes.

But the candles failed to mount with the mounting snow;
The silver bases and then the silver stems
Were buried under the drift, and the drift invaded
The very candles and stems of tender wax,
So that the flames alone remained above the snow,
But the flames persisted, travelling as she travelled,
And the snow touched them not, nor melted they the snow.

Then came the fallow deer with delicate steps,
Printing their steps around her as she stooped,
And their antlers burned with little flames at the tip,
Little daggers of gold at every point,
Pricket and sorel and buck, and the doe with her fawn.

And she knew that she neared the end of the garden path,
And the deer and the buried candles travelled with her,
But still she knew that she would not make an end
Of setting her plants before the shroud came round her.

KATHLEEN MILLAY
1897–1944

Kathleen Millay was the sister of Edna St Vincent. Although a prolific
writer, she never attained her sister's success or popularity. But she
wrote some nine or more volumes of poetry, of which the best known
is probably *The Beggar at the Gate* (1931).

The Masterpiece

So He made woman last – a melody
Kin to the music of the great unknown,
A delicate and monstrous symphony,
Most beautiful in its inharmony;
A work of wondrous dissonance and tone,
Most terrible in its simplicity;
A mighty laughter and a mighty moan
Of harmony and discord and damnation,
Of tears and song, desire and frustration,
To carry on forever and alone

The grim and awful burden of creation –
A thing of tortured flesh and writhing bone,
A beast to bear the load that is His own.

LOUISE BOGAN
1897–1970

Louise Bogan lived largely in New York. Although twice married, she
was an intensely private person whose friendships were extremely
important to her. Her subjects are love and loss, death and dreams,
marriage and grief. In her writing she was never concerned with the
political issues of the day, nor with the depiction of herself. But she
wrote clearly of domestic things, emotions and pain, in a controlled
style, comparable, according to some, with the metaphysical poets. Her
work was much praised during her lifetime and she won many awards,
including the Bollingen Prize (which she shared with Léonie Adams)
and the Academy of American Poets' Award in 1959.

Last Hill in a Vista

Come, let us tell the weeds in ditches
How we are poor, who once had riches,
And lie out in the sparse and sodden
Pastures that the cows have trodden,
The while an autumn night seals down
The comforts of the wooden town.

Come, let us counsel some cold stranger
How we sought safety, but loved danger.
So, with stiff walls about us, we
Chose this more fragile boundary:
Hills, where light poplars, the firm oak,
Loosen into a little smoke.

RUTH PITTER
1897–

Ruth Pitter is an artist and poet, born at Ilford in Essex, the daughter
of two teachers. Her mother was involved in a series of strange
religions, while her father remained a convinced agnostic. She wrote
her first poem aged five, and continued to write throughout her
schooldays and afterwards.

In her forties, she became a confirmed Anglican, and her spirituality
is apparent from her poetry, as is her indestructible optimism. Her
work has been much admired, particularly by other women poets such
as Elizabeth Jennings and Kathleen Raine. She received the Queen's
Gold Medal for Poetry in 1955.

The Sparrow's Skull

Memento Mori. Written at the Fall of France

The kingdoms fall in sequence, like the waves on the shore.
All save divine and desperate hopes go down, they are no more.
Solitary is our place, the castle in the sea,
And I muse on those I have loved, and on those who have loved me.

I gather up my loves, and keep them all warm,
While above our heads blows the bitter storm:
The blessed natural loves, of life-supporting flame,
And those whose name is Wonder, which have no other name.

The skull is in my hand, the minute cup of bone,
And I remember her, the tame, the loving one,
Who came in at the window, and seemed to have a mind
More towards sorrowful man than to those of her own kind.

She came for a long time, but at length she grew old;
And on her death-day she came, so feeble and so bold;
And all day, as if knowing what the day would bring,
She waited by the window, with her head beneath her wing.

And I will keep the skull, for in the hollow here
Lodged the minute brain that had outgrown a fear;
Transcended an old terror, and found a new love,
And entered a strange life, a world it was not of.

Even so, dread God! even so, my Lord!
The fire is at my feet, and at my breast the sword:
And I must gather up my soul, and clap my wings, and flee
Into the heart of terror, to find myself in thee.

Lame Arm

I stood there, by the gate into the yard,
And told Him.
'I'm not so young now, and the work's too hard.'
My bad arm ached, and I began to scold Him.
'Lord,' I said, looking up the diamond air,
'it's ached for years now. I believe You care,
Though I'm a poor thing, and You are the Lord.
If love and pity live in my small brain,
I think they must live in the living Word.

I saw a cage of monkeys at the zoo,
Oh, years ago – and one had hurt his arm.
Didn't know what to do.
He couldn't pray: he didn't know a charm,
But nursed it in a corner, and his eye
Was fixed upon a little patch of sky.
My heart turned over. Oh, I felt to blame!
The creature needed help, and no help came.

Or if I understood
A little better, I could be content.
I do believe that people who are good
Know somehow why these things are sent,
And how to bear them without going bad.
Then pain's no trouble, sorrow isn't sad.

A bigger monkey, Dumbo, had a chain
Hung in his cage, to climb upon, and swing.
So had his next-door neighbour. But the pain
To Dumbo's feebler mind, the dreadful thing,
Was that the friend had got
His chain into a lovely knot:
And poor old Dumbo glowered at his chain,
And hated it for being plain,
And lifted up the end, and made a loop.
And O-so-carefully he drew it down –
Then turned away with a disgusted droop,
And puzzled melancholy frown,
Because no knot appeared. He couldn't do
The headwork – that he had to *pull it through*.

The people round the cage jumped in the air
And ground their teeth and stamped their feet,
And clenched their hands and tore their hair;
And still the poor dumb thing wouldn't be beat.
He did it all day long, and every day. . . .
I couldn't bear to watch, and went away.

If You are Love, You won't mind if I scold.
We laugh when creatures nag. It can be funny.
We *like* their impudence. I know an old
Blackbird I wouldn't sell for any money,
Who curses us to heaps because it's cold.
It's all our fault. We laugh till we are weak.

LÉONIE ADAMS
1899–

Léonie Adams was born in Brooklyn, New York, of parents who encouraged her to write from an early age. From her mother she learned a spirituality and mysticism which may have been the reason for her eventual conversion to the Roman Catholic Church.

Her early poems are slightly mystical, celebrating the joys, and mysteries, of nature. Her later work is more sombre, but still in the mystical tradition. In 1954 she shared the Bollingen Prize with Louise Bogan, a friend and fellow poet.

Early Waking

Four hooves rang out and now are still.
In the dark wall the casements hold
Essential day above each sill,
Just light, and colored like thin gold.
Behind those hooves a drowsy course
All night I rode where hearts were clear,
And wishes blessèd at the source,
And for no shape of time stop here.

No more to raise that lively ghost
Which ran quicksilver to the bone:
By a whim's turn the whole was lost
When all its marrow worth was known.
Ghosts can cast shadows in the breast,
And what was present tears to weep,
Not heart nor mind would bid from rest
As fast as sorrow's, ten years deep.

I travel, not for a ghost's sake,
One step from sleep, and not for one
Left sleeping at my side I wake.
Before bricks rosy with the dawn,
The hooves will sound beyond the light:
There are dark roads enough to go
To last us through the end of night,
And I will make my waking slow.

It was for unconcerning light
That has not fallen on earth, to stare
An instant only out of night
And with night's cloudy character,
Before the laden mind shall slip
Past dream and on to brightmost dream
And fetterless high morning dip
Her two cold sandals in the stream.

Those Not Elect

Never, being damned, see paradise.
The heart will sweeten at its look;
Nor hell was known, till paradise
Our senses shook.

Never hear angels at laughter,
For how comports with grief to know
Wisdom in heaven bends to laughter, laughter,
Laughter upon woe?

Never fall dreaming on celestials,
Lest, bound in a ruinous place,
You turn to wander with celestials
Down holy space.

Never taste that fruit with the soul
Whereof the body may not eat,
Lest flesh at length lay waste the soul
In its sick heat.

STEVIE SMITH
1902–1971

Stevie Smith was born in Hull in Yorkshire, and at the age of three went to London with her mother and sister. They lived with her mother's sister in Palmer's Green. Instead of going to university, she went to be a secretary at Newnes, the magazine publishers, and later in her career she worked as private secretary to Sir George Newnes and Sir Neville Pearson. She learned much about investments in those jobs, leaving a healthy estate that cannot have been exclusively the product of her writing.

She was a committed member of the Church of England, though often strongly critical of it. Her novels show little of her religious beliefs, but her poetry is much more revealing. She was a professed unbeliever, but clearly emerges as a mixture of agnostic, atheist and profound believer, who loved the institution of the Church.

She did not relish the idea of a prolonged death, and was spared it with a rapidly growing brain tumour. She had a curious view of the world, a view imbued with the Church and with Palmer's Green, but she had an intense religious feeling and a fiery quality to her questions of faith that made her hard to argue with, but a delight to read.

I Do Not Speak

I do not ask for mercy for understanding for peace
And in these heavy days I do not ask for release
I do not ask that suffering shall cease.

I do not pray to God to let me die
To give an ear attentive to my cry
To pause in his marching and not hurry by.

I do not ask for anything I do not speak
I do not question and I do not seek
I used to in the day when I was weak.

Now I am strong and lapped in sorrow
As in a coat of magic mail and borrow
From Time today and care not for tomorrow.

Come, Death (1)

Why dost thou dally, Death, and tarry on the way?
When I have summoned thee with prayers and tears, why dost thou
stay?
Come, Death, and carry now my soul away.

Wilt thou not come for calling, must I show
Force to constrain thy quick attention to my woe?
I have a hand upon thy Coat, and will
Not let thee go.

How foolish are the words of the old monks,
In Life remember Death.
Who would forget
Thou closer hangst on every finished breath?
How vain the work of Christianity
To teach humanity
Courage in its mortality.
Who would not rather die
And quiet lie
Beneath the sod
With or without a god?

Foolish illusion, what has Life to give?
Why should man more fear Death than fear to live?

Come, Death (2)

I feel ill. What can the matter be?
I'd ask God to have pity on me,
But I turn to the one I know, and say:
Come, Death, and carry me away.

Ah me, sweet Death, you are the only god
Who comes as a servant when he is called, you know,
Listen then to this sound I make, it is sharp,
Come, Death. Do not be slow.

ANNE MORROW LINDBERGH
1906–

Anne Morrow Lindbergh's career has in many ways been eclipsed by that of her husband, the pioneer aviator Charles Lindbergh. She was educated at Smith College, but after her marriage she learned to fly and to operate the radio, becoming the first woman in America to obtain a glider pilot's licence. She had grown up a very private person, but the publicity attached first to her husband's flights and then to the kidnapping and murder of their baby son, shattered any privacy she had once enjoyed. After the death of their son, the Lindberghs went to Europe to escape the publicity. But they returned in 1939, as the war began.

Throughout her life Anne Lindbergh has produced both fiction and non-fiction prose, and a small collection of poetry. Her subjects are almost always linked to her personal experience, the quiet, sensitive soul plunged into the worst horrors of the real world, with pain and publicity mixed together.

Height

When I was young I felt so small
And frightened for the world was tall.

And even grasses seemed to me
A forest of immensity.

Until I learned that I could grow,
A glance would leave them far below.

Spanning a tree's height with my eye,
Suddenly I soared as high,

And fixing on a star I grew,
I pushed my head against the blue!

Still, like a singing lark, I find
Rapture to leave the grass behind.

And sometimes standing in a crowd
My lips are cool against a cloud.

ELIZABETH BISHOP
1911–1979

Elizabeth Bishop's family history is tragic. Her parents, William Bishop and Gertrude Bulmer, had only three years of married life before he died. Her mother had a nervous breakdown and went to live in a sanatorium, becoming insane. Elizabeth was taken to live first with her maternal grandparents in Great Village, Nova Scotia, then, at the age of six, with her paternal grandparents so that she could go to school in the United States. She was apparently very unhappy in Worcester, Massachusetts, and was also chronically unhealthy with bronchitis and asthma. She records some of this in her poems, which she probably began to write at this time. At Vassar, she became a literary star, and her friendship with the poet Marianne Moore led her to abandon the medical career which she had planned, and concentrate on writing. This she did for the rest of her life. Her style is difficult, her images hard to understand. But her extraordinary insights and her shifting imaginative leaps repay the effort required to appreciate her.

Seascape

This celestial seascape, with white herons got up as angels,
flying as high as they want and as far as they want sidewise
in tiers and tiers of immaculate reflections;
the whole region, from the highest heron
down to the weightless mangrove island
with bright green leaves edged neatly with bird-droppings
like illumination in silver,
and down to the suggestively Gothic arches of the mangrove roots
and the beautiful pea-green back-pasture
where occasionally a fish jumps, like a wild-flower
in an ornamental spray of spray;
this cartoon by Raphael for a tapestry for a Pope:
it does look like heaven.
But a skeletal lighthouse standing there
in black and white clerical dress,
who lives on his nerves, thinks he knows better.
He thinks that hell rages below his iron feet,
that that is why the shallow water is so warm,
and he knows that heaven is not like this.
Heaven is not like flying or swimming,
but has something to do with blackness and a strong glare
and when it gets dark he will remember something
strongly worded to say on the subject.

ANNE RIDLER
1912–

Anne Ridler was born in Rugby, the daughter of a Rugby School
housemaster and his wife. She was educated at Downe House School
and at King's College, London, and then spent six months in Italy.
From 1935 she worked for T. S. Eliot as his secretary, moving on to be
a junior editor in a publishing house. In 1938 she married the printer
Vivian Ridler, by whom she had four children.

She has published nine volumes of poetry on domestic, family and
erotic themes set in a broadly Christian environment. She has also
written several verse dramas in the Eliot tradition, including *Cain,
Henry Bly* and *The Trail of Thomas Cranmer* (1956), the last-named
written for the four hundredth anniversary of Cranmer's martyrdom.

Choosing a Name

My little son, I have cast you out
   To hang heels upward, wailing over a world
   With walls too wide.
My faith till now, and now my love:
   No walls too wide for that to fill, no depth
   Too great for all you hide.

I love, not knowing what I love,
   I give, though ignorant for whom
   The history and power of a name.
I conjure with it, like a novice
   Summoning unknown spirits: answering me
   You take the word, and tame it.

Even as the gift of life
  You take the famous name you did not choose
  And make it new.
You and the name exchange a power:
  Its history is changed, becoming yours,
  And yours by this: who calls this, calls you.

Strong vessel of peace, and plenty promised,
  Into whose unsounded depths I pour
  This alien power;
Frail vessel, launched with a shawl for sail,
  Whose guiding spirit keeps his needle-quivering
  Poise between trust and terror,

And stares amazed to find himself alive;
  This is the means by which you say *I am*,
  Not to be lost till all is lost,
When at the sight of God you say *I am nothing*,
  And find, forgetting name and speech at last,
  A home not mine, dear outcast.

At Richmond

At Richmond the river is running for the city:
Though the tall houses on the hill and hotels
In white paint hint of the cliffs and broader sea,
He cannot falter nor alter from his nature.
Lord, neither let falsity my days dissipate.
I have been weak and injudicious in many things,
Have made my tongue an irritant against my intention,
All quiet but a convalescence after sin,
And have frequently feared. Then forgive
Yet once, bless and beckon to the broken city.

PATRICIA BEER
1924–

Patricia Beer comes of Plymouth Brethren stock. Having begun writing
at the age of ten, she was discouraged by having 'no idea that the real
world could appear in literature.' She was taught at home by her
mother, then passed through the state education system until she went
to university, at Exeter, London and lastly Oxford. She taught at the
University of Padua, then in Rome, and finally at Goldsmith's College,
London. She has written seven or more volumes of poetry; her first,
The Loss of the Magyar, is based on her great-grandfather's death in a
shipwreck. Her several volumes of criticism include work on the
metaphysical poets and a study of nineteenth-century women novelists,
Reader, I married him. She has also written a novel, and continues to
produce a considerable amount of poetry.

Christmas Carols

They say a maiden conceived
Without so much as a kiss
At the time or afterwards.
Gloria in excelsis.

They name the eternal hall
Where we arrive to wine, fire,
Together and loving, but
Dead. *Quam dulcis est amor.*

Although in their description
Every midnight is clear
So that angels can be seen
Without peering, *hilariter,*

We know better in our fear
And avoid most carefully
David's city after dark.
Honor tibi, Domine.

SYLVIA PLATH
1932–1963

Sylvia Plath's unhappy story is so well known it seems almost superfluous to repeat it. She was a Bostonian who came of immigrant stock with an astonishing achievement ethic. She shone, as she was expected to, and her life story informs her poetry in the most vivid way. Her superb achievements – articles in *Seventeen*, and *Mademoiselle*, and a bout as guest editor at *Mademoiselle* – led to exhaustion and a nervous breakdown. After treatment she returned to Smith College, winning top academic awards and a Fulbright Scholarship to Cambridge.

While there, she married the British poet Ted Hughes. She was subsequently tormented by the tearing loyalties to children and home, or poetry and academe. At the age of thirty-one, she committed suicide.

Since her death she has been reassessed, and several critics find her less exciting as a poet than she first appeared. But there is something so strong and vivid in her writing that to my mind she cannot but be classed in the first rank of poets, concentrating on life's crises, and the pain of it all.

Mystic

The air is a mill of hooks –
Questions without answer,
Glittering and drunk as flies
Whose kiss stings unbearably
In the fetid wombs of black air under pines in summer.

I remember
The dead smell of sun on wood cabins,
The stiffness of sails, the long salt winding sheets.
Once one has seen God, what is the remedy?
Once one has been seized up

Without a part left over,
Not a toe, not a finger, and used,
Used utterly, in the sun's conflagrations, the stains
That lengthen from ancient cathedrals
What is the remedy?

The pill of the Communion tablet,
The walking beside still water? Memory?
Or picking up the bright pieces
Of Christ in the faces of rodents,
The tame flower-nibblers, the ones

Whose hopes are so low they are comfortable –
The humpback in his small, washed cottage
Under the spokes of the clematis.
Is there no great love, only tenderness?
Does the sea

Remember the walker upon it?
Meaning leaks from the molecules.
The chimneys of the city breathe, the window sweats,
The children leap in their cots.
The sun blooms, it is a geranium.

The heart has not stopped.

SELECT BIBLIOGRAPHY

Fleur Adcock (ed.): *The Faber Book of Twentieth-Century Women's Poetry* 1987

Arkin, M. and Shellar, B.: *The Longman Anthology of World Literature by Women 1875-1975* London 1989

Brontë, Anne: *The Complete Poems of Anne Brontë*, ed. Clement Shorter, Hodder and Stoughton, London 1920

Brontë, Anne and Emily. *Poems* in. *The Shakespeare Head Brontë*, Oxford 1934

Brontë, Charlotte and Branwell: *Poems* in: *The Shakespeare Head Brontë* Oxford 1934

Browning, Elizabeth Barrett: *Poetical Works* Smith, Elder, London 1907

Buckley, J. H. and Woods, G. B.: *Poetry of the Victorian Period* Scott, Foreman and Co. 1965

Cornford, Frances: *Collected Poems* Cresset Press, London 1954

Cosman, Carol; Keefe, Joan; Weaver, Kathleen: *The Penguin Book of Women Poets* London 1978

Dickinson, Emily: *Complete Poems* ed. Thomas H. Johnson, Little Brown and Co, Boston 1961

Enright, D. J.: *The Oxford Book of Contemporary Verse 1945-1980* 1980

Gardner, Helen: *The Faber Book of Religious Verse* London 1972

Gardner, Helen: *The New Oxford Book of English Verse* Oxford 1972

Linthwaite, Illona: *Ain't I a Woman - a book of women's poetry from around the world* Peter Bedrick Books, New York 1990

Loving, Jerome: *Emily Dickinson - the poet on the second story* Cambridge 1986

Markham, Edwin: *The Book of American Poetry* William H. Wise and Co, New York 1934

Mew, Charlotte: *The Farmer's Bride* London 1921

Mew, Charlotte: *The Rambling Sailor* London 1929

Meynell, Alice: *Poems of Alice Meynell* Burns Oates and Washbourne, London 1923

Milford, H. S.: *The Oxford Book of English Verse of the Romantic Period* 1928

Millay, Edna St Vincent: *Collected Sonnets* Harper and Row, New York 1988

Nesbit, Edith: *The Rainbow and the Rose* Longmans, London 1905

Nesbit, Edith: *A Pomander of Verse* Bodley Head, London 1895

Nicholson, D. H. S. and Lee, A. H. E.: *The Oxford Book of English Mystical Verse* 1927

Palgrave, F. T.: *The Golden Treasury* Collins, London 1959

Emily Pfeiffer: *Sonnets* Field and Tuer, London 1886

Pitter, Ruth: *Collected Poems*, introduced by Elizabeth Jennings, Enitharmon Press, Petersfield 1990

Plath, Sylvia: *Collected Poems* ed. Ted Hughes, Faber 1981

Quiller-Couch, Arthur: *The Oxford Book of English Verse 1250-1918*, 1939

Ricks, Christopher (ed.): *The New Oxford Book of Victorian Verse* 1987

Rossetti, Christina: *Poetical Works*, with memoir and notes by William Michael, Rossetti, Macmillan, London 1904

Scott, P. J. M. *Anne Brontë's Vision* Barnes and Noble, New York 1983

Scrymgeour, D.: *Poetry and Poets in Britain* Edinburgh 1866

Sewall, R. B.: *Emily Dickinson - a collection of critical essays* Prentice Hall, Englewood Cliffs, New Jersey 1963

Skelton, Robin: *Poetry of the Thirties* Penguin, London 1964

Smith, Stevie: *Collected Poems* Penguin, London 1975

Squire, J. C.: *The Cambridge Book of Lesser Poets* 1927

Stetson, Erlene ed.: *Black Sister: Poetry by Black American Women 1746-1980* University of Indiana Press 1981

Weintraub, Stanley: *Four Rossettis - a Victorian Biography* W. H. Allen, London 1978

INDEX OF POETS

INDEX OF FIRST LINES